INTRODUCING
ISSUES WITH
OPPOSING
VIEWPOINTS®

W9-BYZ-789

Internet Journalism and Fake News

Kathryn Roberts, *Book Editor*

GREENHAVEN
PUBLISHING

Published in 2018 by Greenhaven Publishing, LLC
353 3rd Avenue, Suite 255, New York, NY 10010

Copyright © 2018 by Greenhaven Publishing, LLC

First Edition

Articles in Greenhaven Publishing anthologies are often edited for length to meet page requirements. In addition, original titles of these works are changed to clearly present the main thesis and to explicitly indicate the author's opinion. Every effort is made to ensure that Greenhaven Publishing accurately reflects the original intent of the authors. Every effort has been made to trace the owners of the copyrighted material.

Library of Congress Cataloging-in-Publication Data

Names: Roberts, Kathryn, editor.
Title: Internet journalism and fake news / edited by Kathryn Roberts.
Description: New York : Greenhaven Publishing, 2018. | Series: Introducing issues with opposing viewpoints | Includes bibliographical references and index. | Audience: Grades 9–12.
Identifiers: LCCN ISBN 9781534501959 (library bound) | ISBN 9781534502758 (pbk.)
Subjects: LCSH: Online journalism—Juvenile literature. | Journalism—Political aspects—Juvenile literature.. | Journalism—Corrupt practices. | Mass media and public opinion—United States.
Classification: LCC PN4784.O62 I58 2018 | DDC 808/.06607—dc23

Manufactured in the United States of America

Website: http://greenhavenpublishing.com

Contents

Foreword   5

Introduction   7

Chapter 1: How Has the Internet Changed Journalism?

1. Why Anonymity Works on News Sites   10
   Steve Yelvington
2. Citizen Journalists Are Increasingly Important   17
   Demir Hodzic
3. The Internet Has Changed the Media Forever   22
   Matthias Spielkamp
4. Anonymous Sources Present Journalists with an Ethical   31
   Challenge
   Reed Richardson
5. Investigative Reporters Are Harnessing the Power of   40
   Social Media
   Syed Nazakat
6. Balance and Fairness Should Not Be Lost in the Rush   48
   to Break a Story
   Alan D. Abbey

Chapter 2: What Constitutes Fake News?

1. There Is a Difference Between Fake News and   54
   Unverified News
   a1skeptic
2. Comments on News Stories Are Rarely Beneficial   59
   Shan Wang
3. Everyone Should Learn How to Spot Fake News   64
   Eugene Kiely and Lori Robertson
4. Television Is Still the Preferred Source for News   73
   Krysten Crawford

Chapter 3: How Can We Fight Fake News?

1. The Fight Against Fake News Will Be Ongoing   79
   Elia Powers

2. Technology Can Help When Critical Thinking Fails   88
   Victoria L. Rubin, Yimin Chen, and Niall J. Conroy
3. We Must Look Beyond the Message We Want to Hear   93
   Lauren C. Williams
4. Forget Click-Bait and Support Real Journalism   101
   Jeffrey Dvorkin

Facts About Internet Journalism and Fake News   106
Organizations to Contact   108
For Further Reading   111
Index   115

Foreword

Indulging in a wide spectrum of ideas, beliefs, and perspectives is a critical cornerstone of democracy. After all, it is often debates over differences of opinion, such as whether to legalize abortion, how to treat prisoners, or when to enact the death penalty, that shape our society and drive it forward. Such diversity of thought is frequently regarded as the hallmark of a healthy and civilized culture. As the Reverend Clifford Schutjer of the First Congregational Church in Mansfield, Ohio, declared in a 2001 sermon, "Surrounding oneself with only like-minded people, restricting what we listen to or read only to what we find agreeable is irresponsible. Refusing to entertain doubts once we make up our minds is a subtle but deadly form of arrogance." With this advice in mind, Introducing Issues with Opposing Viewpoints books aim to open readers' minds to the critically divergent views that comprise our world's most important debates.

Introducing Issues with Opposing Viewpoints simplifies for students the enormous and often overwhelming mass of material now available via print and electronic media. Collected in every volume is an array of opinions that captures the essence of a particular controversy or topic. Introducing Issues with Opposing Viewpoints books embody the spirit of nineteenth-century journalist Charles A. Dana's axiom: "Fight for your opinions, but do not believe that they contain the whole truth, or the only truth." Absorbing such contrasting opinions teaches students to analyze the strength of an argument and compare it to its opposition. From this process readers can inform and strengthen their own opinions, or be exposed to new information that will change their minds. Introducing Issues with Opposing Viewpoints is a mosaic of different voices. The authors are statesmen, pundits, academics, journalists, corporations, and ordinary people who felt compelled to share their experiences and ideas in a public forum. Their words have been collected from newspapers, journals, books, speeches, interviews, and the internet, the fastest growing body of opinionated material in the world.

Introducing Issues with Opposing Viewpoints shares many of the well-known features of its critically acclaimed parent series, Opposing

Viewpoints. The articles allow readers to absorb and compare divergent perspectives. Active reading questions preface each viewpoint, requiring the student to approach the material thoughtfully and carefully. Photographs, charts, and graphs supplement the articles. A thorough introduction provides readers with crucial background on an issue. An annotated bibliography points the reader toward articles, books, and websites that contain additional information on the topic. An appendix of organizations to contact contains a wide variety of charities, nonprofit organizations, political groups, and private enterprises that each hold a position on the issue at hand. Finally, a comprehensive index allows readers to locate content quickly and efficiently.

Introducing Issues with Opposing Viewpoints is also significantly different from Opposing Viewpoints. As the series title implies, its presentation will help introduce students to the concept of opposing viewpoints and learn to use this material to aid in critical writing and debate. The series' four-color, accessible format makes the books attractive and inviting to readers of all levels. In addition, each viewpoint has been carefully edited to maximize a reader's understanding of the content. Short but thorough viewpoints capture the essence of an argument. A substantial, thought-provoking essay question placed at the end of each viewpoint asks the student to further investigate the issues raised in the viewpoint, compare and contrast two authors' arguments, or consider how one might go about forming an opinion on the topic at hand. Each viewpoint contains sidebars that include at-a-glance information and handy statistics. A Facts About section located in the back of the book further supplies students with relevant facts and figures.

Following in the tradition of the Opposing Viewpoints series, Greenhaven Publishing continues to provide readers with invaluable exposure to the controversial issues that shape our world. As John Stuart Mill once wrote, "The only way in which a human being can make some approach to knowing the whole of a subject is by hearing what can be said about it by persons of every variety of opinion and studying all modes in which it can be looked at by every character of mind. No wise man ever acquired his wisdom in any mode but this." It is to this principle that Introducing Issues with Opposing Viewpoints books are dedicated.

Introduction

Ethical journalism strives to ensure the free exchange of information that is accurate, fair and thorough. An ethical journalist acts with integrity.
> —Preamble, Society of Professional Journalists' Code of Ethics

Today's world has been dominated by the rapid expansion of digital media and the twenty-four-hour news cycle. While this does expand access to a greater population and takes us into a world where journalism is not just for the "elite" crowd with journalism degrees and impeccable credentials, what is the cost? The cost is the rapid rise in the number of dubiously qualified citizen journalists and the dissemination of "fake news" stories. While some "fake news" is easy to ferret out from legitimate news sources, like stories found on the Onion, many "fake news" websites take great pains to look identical to legitimate media entities.

This brings to light a question: what is ethical reporting? The Society of Professional Journalists' Code of Ethics is simple but difficult to follow when many media entities would prefer to be the first to "break" a story, rather than be the first to "get it right." But what damage is done when an inaccurate or unverified story is released and goes viral? Should there be a set standard for journalists and media entities when releasing stories, or is everything superseded by the fact that major media entitics are now privately owned, and the major stakeholders have influence on an individual outlet's editorial policy and the scope of the stories that are published?

And then there are the ethical questions concerning the proliferation of stories published by major media outlets like the AP, Reuters, or the *New York Times* but are authored by freelancers who write under anonymous pen names. Can media outlets be considered "legitimate" when they do not put a name to the stories they publish? How is it appropriate for them to lend credibility to someone not named? And when these published stories are debunked—sometimes in a manner that is embarrassing to the media outlet—what damage does it do to their legitimacy with their continued reliance on anonymous sources who may or may not be peddling in accurate information? Or does the Supreme Court's repeated protection of anonymous users on the internet by way of the First Amendment lend that legitimacy to anonymous writers?

With upward of 44 percent of Americans receiving news of some sort through social media outlets like Facebook, how are consumers supposed to know what news is legitimate and what news is not, when what shows up in a person's newsfeed is dictated by its users determining what news is relevant—whether that news is legitimate or not—along with Facebook's infamous algorithm. Additionally, with Facebook's decision to fire its human Trending Topics curators in 2016, there has been a significant increase in the proliferation of "fake news" stories on that platform. This exacerbates the problem with media consumers only looking for news that conforms to their specific world-view or ideals. These beliefs may not be accurate if the consumers are also influenced by "fake news" or by dubious stories that contain accurate facts, but facts that are cherry-picked to paint a picture that may not be true.

With the rise in pay-per-click advertising, many media outlets turn to questionably sourced content framed by "click-bait" head-lines. Popular listicle website Buzzfeed raised $850 million in 2015 so it could expand into the news-peddling business, but then it published the completely unverifiable "Trump dossier" in January 2017. The highest levels of the US government were briefed on the existence of this dossier, which Buzzfeed ended up deciding to publish so readers could "make up their own minds." Is that an example of good journalism, or are media entities—even the ones popular with the younger generation of media consumers—obligated to just release factual news?

The questions about anonymity on the internet, what constitutes "fake news," how to combat its dissemination, and who is responsible for taking on the websites that treat "fake news" as legitimate are all explored in *Introducing Issues with Opposing Viewpoints: Internet Journalism and Fake News*, shedding light on the multifaceted issue currently facing both journalists and those who consume news media online.

Chapter 1

How Has the Internet Changed Journalism?

Journalistic standards are changing as news has migrated online.

Why Anonymity Works on News Sites

Steve Yelvington

"There is a political value embedded in American journalism, a belief that what we do is essential to sustaining our participatory democracy."

The anonymity of the internet has given the marginalized an ability to speak their opinions without fear of retribution. In the following viewpoint, Steve Yelvington argues that even before the creation of the internet, journalists were writing under pseudonyms and sources were withheld depending on the context of a piece. Even the likes of the Founding Fathers utilized pseudonyms so they could foster revolution. Yelvington was a newspaper reporter and editor and now works on strategy and innovation for Morris DigitalWorks.

AS YOU READ, CONSIDER THE FOLLOWING QUESTIONS:

1. What system was used for internet discussions in the early days?

2. Why would a person want to conceal his or her identity when speaking out on the internet?

3. What is one Supreme Court case mentioned in the viewpoint that upheld the right to speak anonymously?

"Why Anonymity Exists and Works on Newspapers' Web Sites," by Steve Yelvington, the President and Fellows of Harvard College. Reprinted by permission. Published by agreement with the Nieman Foundation for Journalism.

As more newspapers integrate print and online operations, print editors confront a strange new world, in which all of the familiar rules are being broken. In print, letters to the editor must be signed and, in news stories, sources identified, except in specified cases. But when newspapers move online, people in forums, chat sessions, or in comments find themselves engaged in conversations with the Mad Hatter or a Salty Dog.

Mad Hatter? How did we fall down this rabbit hole?

Should newspapers be running their Web sites this way? If we require real names in print, shouldn't we do the same thing online? Aren't there ethical considerations?

It's not that simple. Anonymity and pseudonymity are not merely common to Internet culture, there is a considerable historical, ethical and legal foundation for it.

In its early pre-Web days, most Internet discussions took place on a system called Usenet. Messages commonly were signed with real names and were sent from legitimate research and educational institutions. Exceptions tended to be jokes, such as the April 1, 1984 posting from "Konstantin Chernenko" at "Kremvax," sent long before the network extended into the Soviet Union. Early public online forums, such as the Whole Earth 'Lectronic Link (WELL) and many CompuServe interest groups, also were dominated by real identities. The first newspaper online site I built, at the Star Tribune in Minneapolis, required real names.

But the Web unfolded in a different direction. Those cultures of identity still exist, but they have not grown at the rate of the overall Web. And once the Internet was opened to commercial access and Web sites gained forum capabilities, they quickly attracted users from other cultures more accustomed to using "handles." Many early users were young and came from dial-up bulletin board systems, where some borrowed the identities of comic book heroes such as Judge Dredd. A huge influx of users from America Online, which allowed multiple screen names per account, permanently changed the culture of the Internet.

Once a culture is established, it can be difficult to oppose. "I used to post under my real name … but I felt like the only naked person at a clothing-optional beach," wrote "Salty Dog" in a discussion of this issue at BlufftonToday.com. And for many people, posting under a pseudonym is a protective measure. "When your 13-year-old daughter picks up the phone and hears, 'We're going to burn a cross in your yard,' … you change your attitude toward being 'out there,'" wrote "Wiley Coyote."

Identity: Practice, Ethics and the Law
Earlier this year, I was part of an ethics symposium convened by the Poynter Institute at which a mixed group of Internet media leaders and Poynter faculty tried to clarify a number of ethical issues that are encountered when publishing online. Identity was quickly seen as one of those questions with no simple answers. Instead, it raises more questions: Who is being served? Who is being hurt?

The contextual details are important. Gary Marx, professor emeritus at the Massachusetts Institute of Technology, confronted the ethical questions surrounding anonymity in a 1999 paper, "What's in a Name? Some Reflections on the Sociology of Anonymity." He wrote that "there are many contexts in which most persons would agree that some form of anonymity or identifiability is desirable. But there are others where we encounter a thicket of moral ambiguity and competing rationales and where a balancing act may be called for."

Marx lists a few: liberty and order; accountability and privacy; community and individualism; freedom of expression and the right not to be defamed or harassed. His list continues along those lines and ends with "the desire to be noticed and the need to be left alone"—a conflict we see being played out on MySpace.com today.

Marshall McLuhan observed that communications technologies reshape the world into a global village. Anyone who's ever lived in a small town knows that "everybody knows you" can be suffocating. One middle-aged man, a closeted homosexual in a southern community, wrote to me privately about how he felt a need to express himself in blog postings about gay rights but feared he would lose his job if his employer found out. Another frequent blogger's spouse is employed by the school district that he criticizes vigorously in his postings. For them, anonymity is essential to their ability to participate.

These issues are not unique to the Internet. Indeed, early American journalists often wrote under pen names, particularly in

It may seem like anonymous writing arose as a result of the development of the internet, but journalists have written under false identities as far back as the dawn of the United States.

the Revolutionary period, when the oppressive danger was not merely a tyranny of the majority but a tyranny backed up by military force. Founding Fathers Ben Franklin, John Jay, Alexander Hamilton, and James Madison were among those who occasionally took advantage of pseudonyms. The "seditious libel" of which John Peter Zenger was accused included contributions from a number of anonymous and pseudonymous critics of the Crown.

But how does the law treat such anonymity today? Who is responsible for the content of these postings? Here a common Internet acronym applies: IANAL (I am not a lawyer), so an editor must consult his or her own legal resources and ultimately make an informed decision about risk.

A well-versed lawyer can cite the relevant cases—*Stratton Oakmont, Inc. v. Prodigy, Cubby, Inc. v. CompuServe, Inc.* and *Zeran v. America Online, Inc.* The courts have struck down much of the Communications Decency Act, but the surviving portion includes a statutory "safe harbor" provision for operators of interactive services, and it is clear that Congress intended to promote the development of open conversation by freeing hosts from responsibility for actions taken by guests.

There have been several non-Internet cases in which courts have made it clear that freedom of speech does not come with a hidden price tag of speaker identification. The Electronic Frontier Foundation has said "the Supreme Court has repeatedly upheld the First Amendment right to speak anonymously," citing *Buckley v. American Constitutional Law Foundation, Inc.*, *McIntyre v. Ohio Elections Commission*, and *Talley v. California*. In writing about continuing challenges to anonymity and pseudonymity, a briefing paper written for the conservative Cato Institute calls these ways of protecting one's identity the "cornerstones of free speech."

FAST FACT

Founding Fathers Ben Franklin, John Jay, Alexander Hamilton, and James Madison were among those who occasionally took advantage of pseudonyms.

Even if the law ultimately shields the forum's host, there is a danger of having to defend against nuisance suits and attempts by plaintiffs to intimidate pseudonymous bloggers by demanding disclosure of their identities. In unraveling this knotty problem, it's helpful for editors to ask: Why do newspapers host online conversations, anyway? What are our real goals? To each of these questions, an editor should be able to answer with something other than "so we can get the page views."

Silenced Voices Now Heard

There is a political value embedded in American journalism, a belief that what we do is essential to sustaining our participatory democracy. Editorial and op-ed pages exist to provide a forum for discussion of issues of public interest. Almost without exception, American newspapers require writers of letters or op-ed pieces to identify themselves.

Perhaps this reflects that in our culture order is more valued than freedom and accountability more than privacy, if we return to Marx's list of competing rationales. One result, however, is that many voices are being silenced by fear of social consequences.

Those voices are now being heard on the Internet, where anyone can become a blogger in the two minutes it takes to fill out a form and create an account on any of the many free blog-hosting and social-networking sites. There is no longer a scarcity of places in which public conversation and interaction can happen. Some journalists, such as blogger Jeff Jarvis, have begun to question whether the editorial page has outlived its usefulness. Community conversation will thrive even if every newspaper disappears. Is there a vital and continuing role for newspapers, or even for journalists, to play in providing such a forum for civic and social conversation?

Community conversation can benefit from a framework of goals, ground rules and leadership, and newspapers can perform a real public service by helping provide this. In online forums, five basic identity models exist, and below they are ranked from the "order" to "liberty" ends of the spectrum:

1. Real, verified, published names. It's almost impossible to do this without requiring credit-card transactions.
2. Real names required but not verified. Most "real name" forums on the net today operate this way.
3. Pseudonyms allowed, tied to unpublished real names. Most newspapers with Web registration systems can implement this model easily.
4. Pseudonyms allowed with complete anonymity.
5. Completely open systems—post under any name. This "most free" environment is the most abuse-prone, but a peer-moderation system (such as found on Slashdot.org) can mitigate the damage of an abusive minority.

Among these routes, there is no "correct" path, just a need to consider all these issues and strike a balance. The middle road—public pseudonyms, private identity— might be the optimal, if not ideal, solution. The mask provided by a pseudonym might entice shy persons to contribute, just as they might open up at a costume party.

But as with the real event, it helps if the host knows the identity of everyone in the room; knowing this tends to keep behavior from getting out of hand.

EVALUATING THE AUTHOR'S ARGUMENTS:

Viewpoint author Steve Yelvington argues that anonymity and pseudonymity in journalism are the cornerstones to the preservation of free speech. But for those writers who choose not to write under a pseudonym, what can be done to protect them from online attacks from writers with fake names like the Mad Hatter or Salty Dog?

Viewpoint

2

Citizen Journalists Are Increasingly Important

Demir Hodzic

"Citizen journalism is the basis of democracy that encourages citizens to actively participate in social processes."

In the following viewpoint, Demir Hodzic argues that citizen reporters create and disseminate news because they have a desire to improve society. Not only does the advent of technology open the doors to non-professionals creating news, but it also leads to easier access to both the professional content creator and the hobbyist. This leads to universal access and global relevance, which benefits traditional media and leads to a more accurate and objective society. Hodzic is a writer and graduate of the Izmir University of Economics.

AS YOU READ, CONSIDER THE FOLLOWING QUESTIONS:

1. What is the definition of citizen journalism?

2. What does the author cite as the main guide of mass media today?

3. How do traditional journalists benefit from citizen journalism, according to the author?

"Citizen Journalism and Its Importance," by Demir Hodzic, Flows in Media and Communication, May 23, 2013. Reprinted by permission.

Journalism is constantly struggling with the confidence of his audience, and to retain (or to return) positive reputation, requires adaptation to contemporary needs and demands of media consumers. These changes are imposed on their own, because of this multi-media age, people are in many ways involved in the media world with their comments, uploading photos and video clips. They are no longer just passive observers, but have the opportunity to be active creators and critics. Why then wouldn't the media open the door a little more and allow entry into a whole new realm?

Citizen journalism is the dissemination of information by people who are not professional journalists. Citizen reporters do not do this kind of journalism because it is their job, but because of the way they want to improve society. Citizen journalism is the basis of democracy that encourages citizens to actively participate in social processes.

Jay Rosen, professor at NYU, and member of the Wikipedia advisory board, gives this definition of citizen journalism. "When the people formerly known as the audience employ the press tools they have in their possession to inform one another, that's citizen journalism."

The development of information and communication technologies, especially the Internet, has led to the emergence of citizen journalism, which means the active role of citizens in the process of collecting, reporting, analyzing and disseminating news and information. All citizens create and distribute [news] with the help of mobile phones, the Internet, i-pod, computer, etc. Thanks to digital technology, citizen journalism is universally accessible and globally relevant; it becomes an important part of the content within the traditional media—both public and commercial. It has become an important correction of official sources of information; it helped to create a real and objective view of the world.

When we look at the mass media, they are now mostly privately owned, and their main guide is profit. On the one hand, the media are financed by advertising, and what usually happens is that advertisers and other factors largely influence the editorial policy. The development of technology has in many ways changed the mass media. This is primarily related to the emergence and development of the Internet, which first led to the decline of the popularity of other media, and

The rise of citizen journalism means that more people have an oppportunity to join in on the dissemination of information.

then encouraged the media to change and adapt their content. So today most newspaper companies have web sites, where you are able to read some of the free content from the print edition, or they have portal news. The development of the Internet has allowed newspapers to expand their ways to present content so that now they can in one place publish text, photos, videos, and immediately receive feedback from readers and the like.

As the Internet has expanded the possibilities of previous media, it also allowed ordinary people to express their opinions, and that opinion goes out to millions of people worldwide. An important step happened during the late nineties, when the massive popularity of blogs began. A blog is a type of website that allows users to write on a variety of topics, from intimate diaries to political commentary. Today most newspapers have blogs on their own websites.

YouTube has launched a special channel called YouTube Reporter's Center, where citizens are able to look at a number of video tutorials by some of the leading experts in the field of journalism explaining how to do amateur journalism, i.e. civic journalism. It [covers] a number of topics, from finding ideas for stories, technical implementation, presenting stories, etc. Then there is open YouTube Direct, a channel where media can download or order a few amateur journalism pieces, in which some major media companies such as the San Francisco Chronicle, NPR, the Huffington Post and Politico are involved.

At the last World Blog Expo, held in September this year, the first workshop about citizen journalism was held, for which there was great interest. The fact is that people are increasingly able to actively participate in commenting on current social events. Although it seems that the journalists in this way lose their place, they are actually in a position to improve the quality of their work, thanks to this new type of competition.

FAST FACT

The development of the Internet has allowed newspapers to expand the number of ways it can present content, like text, photos, videos and other interactive content that allows for immediate feedback from readers.

The Guardian has made a system that gives readers insight into the stories that journalists and editors have chosen, but also invites them to participate in choosing the topics they would like to read through their comments and suggestions. Through the columns "News Desk live" readers can follow the daily blog where journalists expose and explain the reasons for selecting a particular story, concerning which will accurately report and why, while all stakeholders are free to express their ideas and suggestions, to make the final product in the better quality. Users can contact the journalist via Twitter (# opennews). Also, under "You Tell Us," readers can comment and suggest ideas for news topics. While most of the media still prefer to close their doors on proposals, and they think about how to charge [for] content that is of interest only for [the] minority, examples such as the *Guardian*, which is a prestigious British newspaper, give a glimmer of hope that journalists still exist primarily because of their audience.

In contemporary society, the role of the media in many ways is changing. Although citizen journalism in some cases is dismissed as unnecessary and too amateur, big media companies have no choice but to support it.

EVALUATING THE AUTHOR'S ARGUMENTS:

Viewpoint author Demir Hodzic notes that media is always changing, especially with the advent of the internet and the rapid expansion of technology. What steps can be taken to ensure that media is and continues to be objective when presented to society?

The Internet Has Changed Media Forever

"In this case we have a situation where people are slow to acknowledge that journalism itself has changed—and for the better."

Matthias Spielkamp

Using journalist Glenn Greenwald's shocking story of whistleblower Edward Snowden as a starting point, Matthias Spielkamp argues the importance of media criticism in the following viewpoint. Additionally, Spielkamp discusses his attempts to teach the importance of using technology to fend off technology, so that journalists can safely gather the information they need to report a complete story, not just the story one country's government may or may not want to showcase. Spielkamp advises public institutions, NGOs, and private companies on online journalism, communication strategies, and information security.

AS YOU READ, CONSIDER THE FOLLOWING QUESTIONS:

1. What journalism-related debate did Glenn Greenwald's story about Edward Snowden spark?

2. Why did Bill Keller say he wouldn't have allowed Greenwald to publish his story?

3. What technologies does the author suggest to protect against surveillance?

"Journalism After Snowden—How the Internet Has Changed the Media," by Matthias Spielkamp, Heinrich Böll Foundation, February 2, 2016. https://us.boell.org/2016/02/02/journalism-after-snowden-how-internet-has-changed-media. The author wishes to thank the Heinrich Böll Stiftung for financial support to write this article.

On June 6, 2013, the British daily newspaper and news website the *Guardian* published an article with the rather inconspicuous headline: "NSA collecting phone records of millions of Verizon customers daily."[1] The sheer number of comments that were subsequently submitted to the newspaper's online version—more than 2,500—was a sign that this would evolve into by far the most important story of the year, if not the blockbuster of the century. The *Guardian*'s story was the beginning of an avalanche of other articles[2] based on the material that U.S. whistleblower Edward Snowden had passed on to a handful of journalists. These ensuing articles became the catalyst for the most important story of the year—a story about the media, the role of journalism in society, and the role of journalists in the media. It is these aspects that I wish to explore in this article.

1. Journalism or Activism?

While the title of this article is "Journalism After Snowden," it could arguably be called "Journalism after Greenwald." We owe it to Glenn Greenwald, the brilliant, defiant and renegade bestselling author and blogger-turned-journalist that Snowden's revelations were made public in the first place. The disclosure, which threw Greenwald into the firing line of intense criticism, personal attacks, and even open hatred by other journalists, also served to launch a long-overdue debate on journalism. That debate is about the line between journalism and activism, about whether it is more important to be "fair and balanced" or truthful. It is also a debate about whether one can even call oneself a journalist while openly taking a stand on an issue. This discussion is by no means new. But recently it has received renewed attention by Dan Gillmor, now the director of the Knight Centre for Digital Media Entrepreneurship at Arizona State University and author of the book *We the Media*, in which he popularized the concept of citizen journalism.[3]

One year after the Lehman Brothers went bankrupt, triggering the 2008 financial crisis, the *Guardian* published an article by Gillmor titled, "The New Rules of News."[4] Describing the coverage of the events leading up to the crisis, Gillmor said that it "reminded me that journalists failed to do their jobs before last year's crisis emerged, and have continued to fail since then." To rectify this, he proposed

22 rules that he would implement if he were head of a news organization. Number 17 states:

> *The more we believed an issue was of importance to our community, the more relentlessly we'd stay on top of it ourselves. If we concluded that continuing down a current policy path was a danger, we'd actively campaign to persuade people to change course. This would have meant, for example, loud and persistent warnings about the danger of the blatantly obvious housing/financial bubble that inflated during this decade.*

So let's take another look at what Glenn Greenwald is doing. Greenwald undoubtedly provided a world-class coverage of the vast body of immensely complex data and files that Edward Snowden provided. Yet, he also explained the implications of his reporting: that we live in a surveillance state, that our governments are violating our laws and even our constitutions, and that the intelligence and security services, such as the NSA in the United States, the GCHQ in Great Britain and many others, are completely out of control.

2. A Disgrace for a Constitutional Democracy, But Not a Surprise

Most of you know what happened to Edward Snowden. The U.S. government seized his passport and thus deprived him of his right to travel. The U.S. government also pressured the governments of Portugal and France to prohibit that an airplane carrying no less than the President of Bolivia fly over their territories over suspicions that Snowden might be on board. They forced the plane to land and searched it, with no trace of Snowden. Many experts consider this a breach of international law. U.S. allies such as Germany were pressured to abstain from granting Snowden asylum. All of this is a scandal, yet hardly surprising. In fact, there's much to learn from what happened to Glenn Greenwald, the journalist who published one shocking story after another about the abuse of power by intelligence services. I am not talking about the fact that people who work with him, such as filmmaker Laura Poitras and security specialist

Journalists often meet with anonymous sources under the cloak of secrecy.

Jacob Appelbaum, are continuously harassed by the U.S. Border Patrol when they enter their own country—to the extent that they felt compelled to settle outside the United States. Nor am I speaking about the fact that the British authorities, with the blessing of high-level government officials, detained Greenwald's partner David Miranda for nine hours at London's Heathrow airport, in clear violation of the controversial British Anti-Terror Law. To sum up: all this is a disgrace for governments who call themselves democratic. Yet, it is to be expected that those who attack the surveillance state will face aggressive repercussions.

3. The Attacks of Journalists on Glenn Greenwald

Less expected, however, was that fellow journalists would attack Greenwald in droves. Greenwald was accused of aiding and abetting a crime because he published the confidential information of

Snowden. He is accused of blurring the boundary between his own opinion and direct reporting. One columnist for the *New York Times* said in a talk show "I'm this close to supporting the imprisonment of Glenn Greenwald—that journalist out there who wants to help [Snowden] escape to Ecuador." Bill Keller, former chief editor of the *New York Times* explained that under his leadership Greenwald would not have been allowed to publish articles on the Snowden data because he was a columnist and not a reporter. And Bob Woodward, known from the Watergate scandal, attacked Greenwald for not having protected his source, and for not having issued a coherent story about the information he received.

I'm a great friend of media criticism. I think it's necessary to monitor the so-called fourth estate and to maintain a degree of control and accountability of an institution that itself is part of a system of control and accountability. However, in this case we have a situation where people are slow to acknowledge that journalism itself has changed—and for the better. That has a lot to do with the advent of blogs and that, these days, anyone can publish online. Yet, this goes beyond the tiresome "bloggers versus journalists" argument, an antagonism of the past.[5] Rather, the question today is how journalism and activism relate to each other, whether journalists are meant to chronicle events or to fight for change.

In countries with a British heritage, especially the United States, the division between reporting and commentary is almost a question of faith. Those who believe in the distinction are journalists, and those who don't are activists. And, in the eyes of a journalist, being an activist is despicable. In their view, they convey facts whereas activists advocate a world view, belief or ideology. While the internet complicated that divide, the Snowden story leaves it on thoroughly shaky ground. The Snowden coverage brought a style of journalism to the forefront that had until then been limited to regional news or the internet. It certainly had not been seen in a 192-year-old British newspaper with a monthly readership of several million people from across the globe.

We are indebted to the reporters of the *Guardian* for choosing and staying with this story in spite of the intense political pressure to which they were subjected. They worked in a legal environment where government was allowed to significantly impede reporting and to force journalists to destroy evidence. And they worked under a government that actually made use of such powers, which are so fundamentally unworthy of a modern democracy. Further, we have to thank the editors of the *Guardian* for permitting someone like Greenwald to continue working on the story, and for doing so in a way that corresponds to Gillmor's vision. Here, we need only think of the above-mentioned rule number 17: "The more we believed an issue was of importance to our community, the more relentlessly we'd stay on top of it ourselves. If we concluded that continuing down a current policy path was a danger, we'd actively campaign to persuade people to change course."

Now—and this is the most recent development in a story already replete with unexpected twists and turns—Greenwald wants to go one step further. He has decided to leave the *Guardian* to start a news organization with money from the billionaire and founder of eBay, Pierre Omidyar. This is a unique opportunity, says Greenwald—and he's no doubt right. Whether this endeavor will succeed and whether such a media venture, once established, won't evolve into a normal newsroom remains to be seen. In any event, I very much look forward to seeing how this experiment unfolds.

4. Journalists and Technology: A Strained Relationship

I have one last item on my list, namely technology. For nearly 15 years (and still, at times, today), I have been a lecturer at universities and have taught at journalism schools. My specialty is everything digital: online research, the use of social media in journalism, how to build a good website, and so on. Whenever I have had the opportunity to design the curriculum myself, I integrate a theme I call "communications security for journalists," although a more apt title would probably be "digital source protection." My aim is to teach participants how to use technology to fend off technology, to use encryption to prevent NSA spyware from infiltrating their email communication, to use hard drive encryption to protect their information if they were to be arrested and interrogated by a "rogue state" such as Great Britain, and to use anonymizing technologies like Tor to allow surfing the web without anyone finding out where they're going to or coming from.

FAST FACT

Ideally the individual's right to privacy is respected and the media can fulfill its mission without being surveilled by an international gang of governments.

My experience was the following: the less repressive the regime of a seminar participant's home country, the less likely they were to be interested in such things. I'm pretty sure that I never, in any of my workshops, convinced a German journalist to use technologies for email encryption actively and permanently. Yet, when I was in Syria a few years prior to the war, I didn't have to convince anyone to use technologies to conceal their internet communication. In fact, the colleagues there were already using them. And now it is us, the journalists coming from nation states deemed to have functioning democracies and rule of law, who have to acknowledge that we haven't been paying attention. We placed confidence in our constitutions, which guarantee the freedom of speech and the press, in the Universal Declaration of Human Rights[6] and in the International Covenant on Civil and Political Rights,[7] which promises to protect the freedom of expression and privacy on the Internet.

The Global Network Initiative states that:

> *States must ensure these protections for anyone within their effective power and control. In many instances they must also protect individuals against violations of their rights by other individuals or companies. Restrictions on rights must be based on published, clear, specific legal rules; serve a legitimate aim in a democratic society; be "necessary" and "proportionate" to that aim; not involve discrimination; not confer excessive discretion on the relevant authorities; and be subject to effective safeguards and remedies.*[8]

We now recognize that it is our own intelligence services and governments who are double-dealing us, spying on us and treating us like criminals and enemies of the state. There were plenty of warning signs, such as the unveiling of the ECHELON surveillance system of the United States in 2001.[9] Most of us ignored those signs, including myself. We must not make that mistake again.

5. Mathematics and Engineering Are Raising the Cost of Surveillance

There is no simple solution to combating surveillance. Mathematics, of course, is always a reliable tool; but, according to cryptography expert Bruce Schneier, only to a certain extent.[10] This is because the surveillance state is a condition, a state of affairs. Neither can technology, alone, protect us against people who have the authority to break into our homes, search our offices and confiscate our mobile phones and computers, who monitor our phone calls and read our emails without having to produce a single piece of evidence of our alleged misconduct. We must use technologies to protect ourselves. I strongly recommend using technologies like PGP, Tor, TLS and IPSec, OTR and open source technologies. Anyone who does not know what all this means needs to educate themselves. There are a number of online and offline tools and manuals out there to introduce neophytes.[11] I also recommend using Disconnect[12] to hide information from Google. Finally, it is important to spread the word. We should make every effort to share what we learn with friends, relatives, and colleagues and to report about it in newspapers, on the radio, on television, in blogs or any other means of information-sharing. Because the more we use these tools, the higher the cost of surveillance. None of these tools provide complete security, because the full protection of privacy or of the reporter's privilege is not possible in a surveillance state. Still, using them is a lot better than surrendering to the otherwise inevitable fate of having all our communications monitored around the clock.

EVALUATING THE AUTHOR'S ARGUMENTS:

Viewpoint author Matthias Spielkamp showcases that in less repressive regimes, journalists are less interested in learning how to use technology to protect their data while doing research. Why is there such variation, and will the parity continue as journalism continues to be influenced by the internet and the development of technology?

Notes

1. Greenwald, Glenn (2013): NSA collecting phone records of millions of Verizon customers daily
2. Greenwald, Glenn et al. (2015): The NSA files. London; http://www.theguardian .com/us-news/the-nsa-files.
3. Gillmor, Dan (2006): We the Media. Sebastopol; http://it-ebooks.info/book/137.
4. Gillmor, Dan (2009): The new rules of news. London; http://www.theguardian.com/ commentis-free/cifamerica/2009/oct/02/dan-gillmor-22-rules-news.
5. Rosen, Jay (2005): Bloggers vs. Journalists is Over. New York; http://archive.press-think.%20org/2005/01/21/berk_essy.html.
6. United Nations (1948): Universal Declaration of Human Rights; http://www.un.org/ en/universal-declaration-human-rights/
7. United Nations (1966): International Covenant on Civil and Political Rights.
8. Brown, Ian/ Korff, Douwe (2012): Digital Freedoms in International Law. Washington, DC; https://globalnetworkinitiative.org/sites/default/files/Digital%20Free-doms%20in%20International%20Law.pdf
9. European Parliament (2011): on the existence of a global system for the interception of private and commercial communications (ECHELON interception system) (2001/2098(INI)), http://www.europarl.europa.eu/sides/getDoc.do?pubRef=-//EP// TEXT+REPORT+A5-2001-0264+0+DOC+XML+V0//EN
10. Schneier, Bruce (2013): NSA surveillance: A guide to staying secure. London; http:// www.theguardian.com/world/2013/sep/05/nsa-how-to-remain-secure-surveillance.
11. Tactical Technology Collective and Front Line Defenders (2015): Security in-a-box. Berlin; https://securityinabox.org
12. https://disconnect.me

Viewpoint

4

Anonymous Sources Present Journalists with an Ethical Challenge

Reed Richardson

"So, like an astronomer trying to detect unseen forces in a distant galaxy, identifying unnamed sources similarly required looking for secondary effects in nearby objects."

In the following viewpoint, Reed Richardson argues that anonymity can bring with it several ethical issues. One significant problem that arises when major media entities grant anonymity to certain sources is that there is no consistent set of "best practices" when evaluating whether or not a source should be considered anonymous. The author notes that each media entity, including the *New York Times*, has its own set of practices. These are constantly amended depending upon the situation and are still not appropriately used to evaluate a source. This can result in a host of conflicts. Richardson is a media critic and writer whose work has appeared in the *Nation* and *AlterNet*.

"Journalism's Dark Matter," by Reed Richardson, FAIR, March 29, 2016. http://fair.org/home /journalisms-dark-matter/. Licensed under CC BY-NC-ND 3.0.

AS YOU READ, CONSIDER THE FOLLOWING QUESTIONS:
1. According to the author, should there be one consistent set of "best practices" for all journalists and media entities to use to evaluate whether a source should be deemed "anonymous"?

2. What did Columbia University students conclude in their survey regarding the *Times*?

3. Why does the author believe reporters need anonymous sources more than ever before?

Journalists face numerous ethical and institutional challenges when doing their job. But none of these challenges lays bare the conflicts and compromises involved in reporting the news quite like the use of anonymous sources.

For a profession predicated on demanding transparency and accountability from others, the practice of granting anonymity serves as an inconvenient reminder of journalism's own messy reality. The implied bargain therein—that the value of the light provided by a source's information outweighs the cost of casting of a shadow over his or her public identity—trades upon both the judgment and authority of the reporter and his or her news organization.

Journalism, as a profession, has a long, sordid history of misusing and abusing anonymous sources. In recent years, news organizations have tried to rein in those excesses with more rigorous ethical rules about their use. The Society of Professional Journalists has published recommended best practices, but newspapers and media outlets routinely pick and choose which of these they will follow—if they follow any of them at all—and cobble together their own in-house guidelines. More often than not, however, these anonymity rules work in a prescriptive rather than normative fashion and are reactive in nature, narrowly tailored to correct the latest embarrassing mistake.

The *New York Times* is no exception. In fact, the paper just unveiled yet another update to its rules on granting anonymity earlier this month (3/15/16) after two major anonymous sources stories blew up in the paper's face last year. This follows more than a decade of false starts and half-measures reaching back to 2004, when the paper finally published an explicit confidential news sources policy after its reputation was publicly battered by the twin scandals of Jayson Blair's fabulism and its credulous Iraqi WMD coverage. But only a year later, the paper saw the need to further tighten its guidelines, the effect of which "created the potential to profoundly alter the role of confidential sources in the *Times*' newsroom," according to the (very optimistic) then-*Times* public editor, Byron Calame (11/20/05).

Just two years after that rosy assessment, however, a survey by Columbia University Journalism School students found that the paper had cut down on the use of anonymous sources, but that only one in five instances met the paper's own citation standards. In 2009, Craig Whitney, the *Times* standards editor at the time, told Clark Hoyt, Calame's successor as public editor (3/22/09), an all too familiar tale: "The bar should be far higher than it is before a reporter puts an anonymous quote in and before an editor lets it stay in." But as FAIR documented (*Extra!*, 11/11), the *Times* consistently failed to live up to its own standards in the years following that pronouncement as well.

And so, nearly 12 years after the *Times*' first public editor, Daniel Okrent (5/4/04), condemned the "toxic" effect of unnamed sources in the paper, the *Times* continues to struggle with endemic abuses of anonymity. Current public editor Margaret Sullivan acknowledged as much in a column at the end of 2014 (12/29/14):

> One thing is certain: Anonymity continues to be granted to sources far more often than a last-resort basis would suggest.... But 2015 is another year to try to root out what some have called the "anonymice"—and the dubious rationalizations they travel with.

So after all these years of newsroom memos and executive rhetoric, I wondered, what exactly does a year's worth of anonymous sources now look like at the *New York Times*? The answer, it turns out, is a journalistic amalgam of frustrating ambiguity and mind-numbing repetition, with moments of stunning negligence and unmitigated triumph mixed in. Far from being a "last resort," however, anonymous sources remain stubbornly common within the paper, and were,

The New York Times has revised its policy on anonymous sources several times in recent years. The news organization has come under fire for its practices in the past.

notably, even more likely to be found lurking among high-profile and front-page stories.

If you're looking for a definitive total of anonymous-source articles published by the *Times* last year, you won't find it here. Or anywhere. After sorting and categorizing tens of thousands of data points and poring over hundreds of individual articles, blog posts and columns, I can only say with high confidence that the number of anonymous-source stories published by the *Times* in 2015 approached 6,000, out of roughly 88,000 individual articles, blog posts and columns from both the paper and wire services. But I'm convinced the exact number is unknown by any mere mortal (or editor on Eighth Avenue).

That's not to say that much of the *Times'* anonymity output couldn't be quantified. But to try to conduct a comprehensive census across 12 months of its editorial output is to realize the insidious nature of anonymous sources and the limitations they impose. So, like an astronomer trying to detect unseen forces in a distant galaxy, identifying unnamed sources similarly required looking for secondary effects in nearby objects.

Fortunately, the *Times'* confidential source guide establishes a clear policy for just such a thing. Whenever *Times* reporters cite an anonymous source, they are *supposed* to clearly spell out in an adjacent explanation that source's relevant background and motivations for remaining anonymous. (Note my emphasis on "supposed," which I'll address later.) The accompanying phrasing that the *Times* and other news organizations have adopted for this—"upon condition of anonymity" or "insisted upon/requested anonymity"—thus became a guiding light for my anonymous source research.

[...]

In one respect, this high-profile status makes sense. Blockbuster revelations of wrongdoing often necessitate using unnamed sources to get an important story out, and last year the *Times* had several remarkable examples of intrepid reporting worthy of the front page. Consider the fantastic DealBook series on widespread arbitration abuse, which heard from an unnamed "cruise ship employee" who was cruelly prohibited from suing her employer after she was drugged and raped by fellow crew members. Without the key details provided

Anonymously sourced stories in the *New York Times*, by section

| Business 26% | Foreign 41% | Metro 13% | National 10% | Sports 3% | Other 7% |

Source: Fair.org

by numerous anonymous sources inside the U.S. military, the chilling account of the limited oversight given to Seal Team Six's secret kill missions would not have been possible. Likewise, the sweeping exposé of the nail salon industry, though controversial, drew much of its narrative strength from confidentially giving voice to many voiceless immigrant women being preyed upon by ruthless salon owners.

Many, many more of 2015's anonymous-source front-page stories were not like the above, however. For every confidential whistleblower quoted, there were dozens more unnamed "American officials" to be found; time and again, the powerful enjoyed the privilege of anonymity orders of magnitude more often than the powerless. All too often, the *Times'* front page resembled a journalistic dumping ground for anonymous source-driven ego scoops, trial balloons, buck-passing and what University of London professor and media critic Aeron Davis calls "inter-elite communication."

Moving beyond this first orbit, there was an even larger ring in the anonymous-source solar system, which consisted of stories reported and written by wire services but published by the *Times*. (A majority of these were breaking news stories posted only on the *Times* website.) Last year, the combined total of these Associated Press, Reuters and other wire service stories came to more than 3,800. Combined with the total of *Times*-authored articles, the full-year figure of anonymity rises to more than 5,300 print or online articles—or nearly 15 anonymous-source stories every day.

Anonymity at the Granular Level

But even if the *Times* has made notable strides toward reining in its reliance on anonymity, it doesn't mean gross abuses of the practice don't still occur on a regular basis. One of the most common of these lingering problems involves a routine lack of transparency in the justifications for granting anonymity. In a *Times* internal memo on anonymous sources from 2010, standards editor Phil Corbett warned against disrespecting the reader by not taking this step seriously. "Pat, formulaic expressions of why an anonymous source wants to be anonymous are probably worse than no explanation at all," he wrote. "Let's stop using such rote formulas as 'because he/she was not authorized to speak …' or 'because of the sensitivity of the issue.'"

Good advice, to be sure, since these tautological excuses do little to inform the reader. Nevertheless, 2015 still saw far too many examples where this guidance was ignored. For example, in January of last year, nearly half of the 113 declared "anonymity" *Times* stories fail to live up to this standard, either because they failed to give a justification or because they employed the circular logic Corbett dismissed. For the whole year, 190 stories gave no anonymity justification whatsoever and 133 more stooped to the "not authorized to talk to the media" crutch. To be fair, the latter numbers would mark an improvement from a few years ago, as Corbett's 2010 memo also noted the paper had used the "not authorized…" reason nearly 300 times in the year prior.

Of course, adhering to *Times* policy for justifying a source offers no guarantee the anonymity was actually justifiable. Indeed, 2015 offered up plenty of examples of the sometimes absurd, sometimes contrived reasons that reporters can give for granting anonymity: "afraid of looking bad," "always wanted to be an anonymous source," "because he hoped to be asked to play [golf with President Obama] again," "he did not want to affect his company's stock price by commenting publicly on the state of the industry," "to discuss his clients' fluctuating moods," "the uncertainty over [New York Assembly Speaker Sheldon] Silver's fate and legacy," "as is customary before meetings of eurozone ministers" and, one of my favorites: "to treat a delicate situation with a level of candor frowned upon in politics."

That last, precious excuse came from a May 2015 story where anonymous aides and allies of Chris Christie dared to acknowledge what was already blindingly obvious to everyone else—that the highly unpopular New Jersey governor had a slim chance of becoming the Republican presidential nominee. And yet anonymity was still granted by the *Times* to report such banalities.

FAST FACT

In 2015, the combined total of anonymous AP, Reuters, and other wire service stories came to more than 3,800. Combined with the *Times*-authored articles, the full-year figure of anonymous stories was 5,300, or nearly 15 anonymous-source stories every day.

By contrast, it's hard to beat this as one of 2015's best justifications for anonymity: "because he did not want to be identified admitting to a war crime," which could be found in a chilling, on-the-ground account of an Iraqi militia whose members were interrogating and then summarily killing captured ISIS fighters.

While the "how" and "why" of anonymity presented one set of problems in 2015, the "who" of the anonymous sources presented yet another. Perhaps no *Times* reporter better exemplified this dilemma than Eric Schmitt. Assigned to cover sometimes impenetrable beats like the war against ISIS and the US's classified drone program, Schmitt, a two-time Pulitzer Prize winner, topped the list in anonymous source usage in nearly every category in 2015. He led the paper in total number of declared anonymous–source stories (62), percentage of anonymity stories compared to his total output (57 percent; 62 out of 108 stories), and number of front-page anonymous–source stories (36).

The truth is reporters need anonymous sources more than ever. There have never been more secretive government agencies, egregiously powerful corporations or corrupt, compromised politicians in need of exposing to sunlight. Holding them all accountable, though, will require a journalism that doesn't cheapen or delegitimize the role of whistleblowers by associating their critical voices with pointlessly secret trivia or commodified spin from officialdom. In the conclusion of *On the Condition of Anonymity*, Matt Carlson offered up a simple but profound question about the use of anonymity in the news: "In the end, does it serve journalists, sources or the public?" After studying a full year of anonymity at the *Times*, it's clear much work still needs to be done to ensure that the answer is the latter.

EVALUATING THE AUTHOR'S ARGUMENTS:

This viewpoint's author argues that the *New York Times* over-uses anonymous sources and is also inconsistent when considering which sources can be deemed anonymous. Since the *Times'* stance on using anonymous sources is not likely to change, how can it and other media entities keep their anonymous sources accountable?

Investigative Reporters Are Harnessing the Power of Social Media

"The internet has not replaced getting out, gathering information and documents, and talking face-to-face to people during research."

Syed Nazakat

Social media has changed how people interact with the news. Therefore, the news must adapt to these changes. In the following viewpoint, Syed Nazakat shows that modern journalists are now grappling with how to integrate new social media and technology into their investigative reporting. The fact remains that the importance of objective, believable reporting is ensuring that journalists—users of social media or no—remain justifiably transparent with their readership. Nazakat is an award-winning journalist and editor-in-chief of the Centre for Investigative Journalism.

AS YOU READ, CONSIDER THE FOLLOWING QUESTIONS:

1. How can social media help journalists break stories?

2. Why might investigative journalists refuse to use social media to assist in their reporting?

3. What are the three Cs of journalism?

"Social Media and Investigative Journalism," by Syed Nazakat, the International Consortium of Investigative Journalists, August 15, 2012. Printed with friendly permission of the Konrad-Adenauer-Stiftung.

The rise of the internet in the early 1990s has changed the process of newsgathering for general and investigative reporting in particular—in the way it reaches out to audiences and the way news and information is gathered and distributed.

Social media is largely defined as a group of internet-based applications built on the web, allowing the creation and exchange of content. The internet has not replaced getting out, gathering information and documents, and talking face-to-face to people during research, but in a time of information overload, the internet has made readers and viewers a part of the news gathering process.

The aim is to use social media as a platform to bring in information and at the same time make media more interactive, informative and entertaining.

The growth of the internet and a changing media landscape raises immediate questions for media and journalists: How should we use and integrate new social media technology, like Facebook and Twitter, into investigative reporting, and what are the new models for web-based newsrooms?

Social Media as a Complement to Old Methods

On 13 October 2011, around 500 investigative journalists from more than 50 countries met at the Global investigative Journalism conference in the Ukrainian capital of Kiev. They discussed the use of cross-border investigative stories, undercover reporting, multimedia and new storytelling strategies. All agreed that social media platforms have changed the way people interact with the news, and that more than ever, people are eager and capable of responding to news.

While some shared how useful the social media could be in investigative reporting, others were forthcoming about the limitations of social media. However, all agreed that social media tools are an aid to old-fashioned shoe-leather investigative reporting and if reporters are not currently benefitting from the different tools of social media, they are missing out on something very important. Almost all of the participants at the Kiev conference had Facebook and Twitter accounts.

From my own experience about how useful social media could be in investigative reporting, I recall that in 2010 I was working on a major investigative story about the CIA's covert operations in India. It

More people than ever are getting their news from online platforms, specifically social media platforms. Journalists and media companies have been forced to adapt.

was a complex story as there was nothing in the public domain which could provide a lead. It was hard to get the right people to speak, and particularly those who had worked or dealt with the CIA. While I was working on the story I received an email alert through a social media network about a conference on the US Strategy for Pakistan and Afghanistan, which was being held in Washington. One of the speakers at the conference was Robert Grenier. He was introduced as an intelligence expert. I "googled him" and found that Grenier was one of the most experienced spies to run the far-flung US intelligence network and he had also served as the CIA station chief in Islamabad, Pakistan. Within the agency he was known by his nickname, Bob. In an email I asked him whether he would be available for an interview with our magazine. Bob, who is retired and lives in Virginia, agreed to an email interview. It was a scoop for our magazine. Thanks to the

Facebook community, it was perhaps the first time that a top CIA official had spoken to an Indian publication.

Facebook helped me again in another cross-border major story. It was early 2011. I was planning a reporting assignment on the al-Qaeda rehabilitation camp in Saudi Arabia. I wondered how it might be possible to break through the net of silence and mystery, and whether I could tell the story of young Arabs who were returning to normal life after joining a global terrorist organisation. I wanted to interview someone who had seen, met, or been close to the al-Qaeda chief, Osama bin Laden. I made a number of email requests and phone calls to my friends in Riyadh, but there was no news. My Arab fixer also failed to find any former al-Qaeda men. A journalist friend in Riyadh said that he knew one such fellow but he was unable to be traced. Later I approached the Saudi Arabia ambassador in Delhi, Faisal al-Trad, for help. He kindly helped with the logistic support in Saudi Arabia but he too could not provide a contact. Exhausted by weeks of hunting, I was feeling disappointed. Then, I finally heard about Jamal Khashoggi through a Facebook friend. Jamal is a senior Arab journalist who had fought alongside Afghans and other Arabs, including Osama bin laden, in the war against the former Soviet Union in the 1980s. I was pleased to find him on both Facebook and Twitter. Later, I met him in Riyadh and he spoke about his days with Osama. His views enriched our story and we were able to produce a major report on al-Qaeda.

Investigative journalists such as the *Guardian's* Paul Lewis have demonstrated the value of the network effect in several investigative stories. In one of his recent assignments he investigated the mysterious death of Angolan refugee Jimmy Mubenga on British Airways Flight 77. To find witnesses of what took place on the flight, Lewis tweeted from his account, asking for anyone who was on the flight and saw what happened. He soon received several responses, including one from a man who tweeted that: "I was also there on Ba77 and the man was begging for help and I now feel so guilty that I did nothing." Then, in a breakthrough, he received a phone call from a man in Angola, who was an eye-witness to the killing. In another story, Paul investigated the death of Ian Tomlinson at the g20 protests in London, through Twitter. Paul obtained twenty reliable witnesses who could be placed on a map at the time of the incident—and only one of them had come from the traditional journalistic tool of a contact number in his notebook.

Yet, one of the biggest challenges for many investigative journalists is opening up to the community in the first place. Many investigative journalists do not use social media because they are convinced that if they use social media sites like Facebook or Twitter, other reporters will steal their story or source. David E. Kaplan, editor-at-large at the Organized Crime and Corruption Reporting Project (OCCRP), echoes the anxiety about the use of social media. "No reporter should be putting out sensitive sources or stories they're worried about losing," he said. "Sure, you want tips and public support and interest. But it's a competitive, risky, and sometimes dangerous business, and there are plenty of reasons for investigative journalists to take great care with what they're making public in the course of an investigation."

The question is then how to deal with this situation? Sheila Coronel, director of the Stabile Center for Investigative Journalism, at Columbia University, believes social media is a tool in the journalist's toolkit and that reporters should decide what tools would fit their stories best. "There is no single rule that applies to all. This is something that should be decided on a case-by-case basis. If using social media might expose confidential sources or blunt a news organisation's competitive edge, then journalists may opt to not publicise an ongoing investigation. On the other hand, making public an ongoing project can have advantages, such as, for example, encouraging readers, experts or whistleblowers to contribute information, sources, leads, and tips."

One of the areas where social media can also be helpful is to track an individual, or a story, on the web. Following newsmakers is a key way of tracking news on social networks. Individuals provide colour and context to investigative stories. The information on their Facebook and Twitter accounts about their educational background, family, circle of friends, professional associations, their likes and dislikes, and even their travel records can add to the public knowledge of an individual's private activities. Today people are putting so much information about their private lives on the internet, that it has encouraged intelligence agencies like the CIA to monitor social media websites to collect intelligence. It is all a far cry from the historical spy-work process, which traditionally focused on human intelligence. In terrorism-related investigative stories too, it has been often found that terrorists have a penchant for social media sites. Their postings, pictures and personal information on Facebook, Twitter and other social media platforms may provide an important breakthrough for a story.

The Social Media Scoop

More importantly, when individuals make newsworthy statements on social networks it may give a clue and direction to a story. In some newsrooms, as a part of their reporting beat, reporters are already monitoring government websites for clues about the government's day-to-day activities or subtle changes in policies that in reality may have a larger impact on the public. Who knows when a reporter might get a scoop from the world of social media that may otherwise have been overlooked or was more difficult to effectively track in the past? In India, for example, many politicians, government officials and businessmen are on Facebook and Twitter. They often tweet about their life, work and travel and their tweets often find a place on the front page of the newspaper.

The internet also offers more access to global communities of interest, which may provide alternate sources of information. On the web, there are numbers of reliable, dedicated groups and individuals, sharing important information.

The role of social media does not end with the completion of a story. Today, social media is also being used to promote investigative stories and journalism. Paul Cristian Radu, executive director of the Organized Crime and Corruption Reporting Project (OCCRP), says they are using social media sites to promote their investigative work, and to reach a wider audience. OCCRP's goal is helping people of the region to better understand how organised crime and corruption affect their lives. In addition to the stories, OCCRP is building an online resource centre of documents related to organised crime, including court records, laws, reports, studies, company records and other public documents that will be an invaluable resource centre for journalists and the public alike. "At this point we're mainly using social media to promote our investigative work, to reach a wider audience. We are also using it, although to a limited extent, for crowd-sourcing information," said Paul. He believes that spot.us could be a relevant model once an investigative organisation manages to build a crowd-sourcing community.

The US-based investigative news web portal, ProPublica, led by Paul Steiger, the former managing editor of the *Wall Street Journal*, is experimenting with the same formula. It wants to design and implement social efforts to deepen and advance ProPublica's reporting. It wants to grow its Facebook presence and day-to-day oversight of @ProPublica and #Muckreads, and to integrate social media with its data features. Its website claims that "our Twitter and Facebook use will challenge your ability to spot the crucial or buried bits of news stories, and present them in a clickable and shareable manner." It is also planning a blog which will be aimed at aggregating any noteworthy investigative reporting that it can find that day.

An investigative story, even when it is published, often requires some transparent finessing to establish a sense of trust and credibility in the reporting process that took place—especially with controversial or sensitive topics. Social media tools come in handy here as these are useful for opening a dialogue about the story after it is published. The *Wall Street Journal*, for example, in its recent series on digital privacy, created a Twitter account that provided information on the topic and answered questions from readers. Because the series of stories created a lot of discussion and curiosity, this was an innovative way for the journal to help address readers' questions.

It is hard to overlook the fact that any modern media operation today needs to have a social media element, and journalists need to be far more interactive with the public than ever before. To maintain transparency, reporters are expected to use their full name and professional title in social biographies; include language to indicate that links do not equal endorsements and the news outlets must provide fact-check information on social networks in the same way that they verify any other information for print.

The point is that when using social networks for reporting, it is important that a journalist should be as transparent as possible about sources and methods, so that audiences can make their own assessments of the information. In short, I suggest that journalists should always remember the three Cs—content, clarity and credibility. No matter what kind of latest and sophisticated technology you use, it is the content which will remain the king. For content to have a value it should be clear, to attract and sustain the interest of readers. And at the end of day it is the credibility which separates journalism from propaganda and fiction. Remember without credibility, journalism is a lie.

EVALUATING THE AUTHOR'S ARGUMENTS:

Syed Nazakat, the author of this viewpoint, contends that investigative journalists endeavor to be transparent and credible, no matter what kind of technology they choose to either use or not use. In this era that is dominated by social media, is it mandatory that social media be used to supplement investigative journalism? Why or why not?

"Are fairness and balance achieved only when all of the disparate pieces of a breaking news story are consolidated and organized into a coherent whole?"

Balance and Fairness Should Not Be Lost in the Rush to Break a Story

Alan D. Abbey

With the advent of the twenty-four-hour news cycle, journalists are under mounting pressure to be the first to "break" a story. But there are numerous ethical considerations to make before "pulling the trigger" on a story. In the following viewpoint, Alan D. Abbey poses important questions about the fundamentals of balance and fairness in journalistic reporting. There are many questions based in the values of ethics, all of which are heavily contested and have few clear answers. Abbey is director of internet and media at the Shalom Harman Institute in Jerusalem.

AS YOU READ, CONSIDER THE FOLLOWING QUESTIONS:

1. What actions should be taken when a journalist strives to be the first to "break" a major story?

2. What kind of damage is caused by a "breaking story" that is released without all the facts?

3. What check on balance does the author mention?

The Meaning of Balance and Fairness

Balance and fairness are classic buzzwords of journalism ethics: In objective journalism, stories must be balanced in the sense of attempting to present all sides of a story. Fairness means that a journalist should strive for accuracy and truth in reporting, and not slant a story so a reader draws the reporter's desired conclusion.

Some critics argue that journalists never succeed in being completely balanced and fair—in telling all sides of a story. News coverage often represents the voices of those only on both extremes of the spectrum or voices of those who are the most powerful. Election coverage is a good example of this. In many countries, candidates from non-mainstream parties garner little news coverage. This, critics argue, leads to candidates never building recognition and, therefore, never getting elected.

Seeking Comment

In an effort to ensure fairness, what efforts should be made to reach people for comment on a story that mentions them? If they can't be reached, when should a journalist go with the story, understanding the competitive pressures in the marketplace? In the interest of transparency, how far should a journalist go in explaining the efforts made to contact the person?

Breaking News

Journalists are often criticized for lack of balance and fairness in breaking news situations. Some media publish uncorroborated Twitter feeds that, at best, tell a story only in pieces. An accusation against a prominent individual may be posted online before a response is solicited or before the accused may even have been informed of the comment.

Media critics and watchdogs of all political persuasions are quick to jump on such reports in their zeal to prove a lack of fairness and balance. Do they have a point? Are fairness and balance achieved only when all of the disparate pieces of a breaking news story are consolidated and organized into a coherent whole? What of the damage

Society of Professional Journalists

C:SPJ:DE *of* ETHICS

PREAMBLE

Members of the Society of Professional Journalists believe that public enlightenment is the forerunner of justice and the foundation of democracy. Ethical journalism strives to ensure the free exchange of information that is accurate, fair and thorough. An ethical journalist acts with integrity.

The Society declares these four principles as the foundation of ethical journalism and encourages their use in its practice by all people in all media.

SEEK TRUTH AND REPORT IT

Ethical journalism should be accurate and fair. Journalists should be honest and courageous in gathering, reporting and interpreting information.

Journalists should:

▶ Take responsibility for the accuracy of their work. Verify information before releasing it. Use original sources whenever possible.

▶ Remember that neither speed nor format excuses inaccuracy.

▶ Provide context. Take special care not to misrepresent or oversimplify in promoting, previewing or summarizing a story.

▶ Gather, update and correct information throughout the life of a news story.

▶ Be cautious when making promises, but keep the promises they make.

▶ Identify sources clearly. The public is entitled to as much information as possible to judge the reliability and motivations of sources.

▶ Consider sources' motives before promising anonymity. Reserve anonymity for sources who may face danger, retribution or other harm, and have information that cannot be obtained elsewhere. Explain why anonymity was granted.

▶ Diligently seek subjects of news coverage to allow them to respond to criticism or allegations of wrongdoing.

▶ Avoid undercover or other surreptitious methods of gathering information unless traditional, open methods will not yield information vital to the public.

▶ Be vigilant and courageous about holding those with power accountable. Give voice to the voiceless.

▶ Support the open and civil exchange of views, even views they find repugnant.

▶ Recognize a special obligation to serve as watchdogs over public affairs and government. Seek to ensure that the public's business is conducted in the open, and that public records are open to all.

▶ Provide access to source material when it is relevant and appropriate.

▶ Boldly tell the story of the diversity and magnitude of the human experience. Seek sources whose voices we seldom hear.

▶ Avoid stereotyping. Journalists should examine the ways their values and experiences may shape their reporting.

▶ Label advocacy and commentary.

▶ Never deliberately distort facts or context, including visual information. Clearly label illustrations and re-enactments.

▶ Never plagiarize. Always attribute.

MINIMIZE HARM

Ethical journalism treats sources, subjects, colleagues and members of the public as human beings deserving of respect.

Journalists should:

▶ Balance the public's need for information against potential harm or discomfort. Pursuit of the news is not a license for arrogance or undue intrusiveness.

▶ Show compassion for those who may be affected by news coverage. Use heightened sensitivity when dealing with juveniles, victims of sex crimes, and sources or subjects who are inexperienced or unable to give consent. Consider cultural differences in approach and treatment.

▶ Recognize that legal access to information differs from an ethical justification to publish or broadcast.

▶ Realize that private people have a greater right to control information about themselves than public figures and others who seek power, influence or attention. Weigh the consequences of publishing or broadcasting personal information.

▶ Avoid pandering to lurid curiosity, even if others do.

▶ Balance a suspect's right to a fair trial with the public's right to know. Consider the implications of identifying criminal suspects before they face legal charges.

▶ Consider the long-term implications of the extended reach and permanence of publication. Provide updated and more complete information as appropriate.

ACT INDEPENDENTLY

The highest and primary obligation of ethical journalism is to serve the public.

Journalists should:

▶ Avoid conflicts of interest, real or perceived. Disclose unavoidable conflicts.

▶ Refuse gifts, favors, fees, free travel and special treatment, and avoid political and other outside activities that may compromise integrity or impartiality, or may damage credibility.

▶ Be wary of sources offering information for favors or money; do not pay for access to news. Identify content provided by outside sources, whether paid or not.

▶ Deny favored treatment to advertisers, donors or any other special interests, and resist internal and external pressure to influence coverage.

▶ Distinguish news from advertising and shun hybrids that blur the lines between the two. Prominently label sponsored content.

BE ACCOUNTABLE AND TRANSPARENT

Ethical journalism means taking responsibility for one's work and explaining one's decisions to the public.

Journalists should:

▶ Explain ethical choices and processes to audiences. Encourage a civil dialogue with the public about journalistic practices, coverage and news content.

▶ Respond quickly to questions about accuracy, clarity and fairness.

▶ Acknowledge mistakes and correct them promptly and prominently. Explain corrections and clarifications carefully and clearly.

▶ Expose unethical conduct in journalism, including within their organizations.

▶ Abide by the same high standards they expect of others.

The SPJ Code of Ethics is a statement of abiding principles supported by additional explanations and position papers (at spj.org) that address changing journalistic practices. It is not a set of rules, rather a guide that encourages all who engage in journalism to take responsibility for the information they provide, regardless of medium. The code should be read as a whole; individual principles should not be taken out of context. It is not, nor can it be under the First Amendment, legally enforceable.

The Society of Professional Journalists Code of Ethics is a guide by which journalists abide voluntarily in this time of changing journalistic practices.

done in the interim? How much must a journalist try for fairness and balance while on deadline?

"False Balance"

In the case of balance, one question a journalist must ask is whether she is simply providing "false balance" by presenting an opposing point of view if the facts are presumably well known, as is the case with evolution. That is,

every time a journalist mentions evolution, must he give equal space to those who don't believe in evolution? Polls show a large number of Americans don't believe in evolution, and "creation science" is gaining hold in some school curricula. Should those facts be ignored, even if evolution is a fact?

Another major issue in the news is global warming. Although there is overwhelming consensus among scientists that global warming is occurring, a recent study by Yale University notes that only 63 percent of Americans believe global warming is happening.

So, must a journalist writing about weather trends make a nod to the "debate" about global warming? What if the story is about a debate on government actions to combat global warming? Must a reporter who quotes a government official who says she doesn't believe in global warming "balance" that comment by saying there is a scientific consensus that global warming is a true phenomenon? Does the journalist need to provide a source for that comment, even though it is widely accepted?

Balance and Fairness in Point-of-View Journalism

If you and your news organization don't subscribe to an impartial model of reporting but rather acknowledge that you lean toward a particular political or social point of view, can you throw balance out the window? Or do you still have an ethical obligation to represent multiple perspectives? Do you feel comfortable with the idea that the "other side's" argument is available in other outlets—e.g. that a politically progressive publication isn't obligated to offer a conservative argument on an issue because that argument is presented by conservative publications? This has been standard operating procedure for journals of opinion for decades. Many people, however, tend to gravitate toward media that reinforce their beliefs, and they are not exposed to alternate positions. Therefore, does presenting only "one side" serve the public interest? Does the "echo chamber" effect, in fact, obligate journalists to acknowledge the other side—or sides—of an argument?

One check on balance is reader reaction. Comments on content can help you identify slanted coverage. Certainly pressure groups can jam up your comment sections with "flaming" posts of little value. But reader reaction can also provide early warnings of actual balance problems.

EVALUATING THE AUTHOR'S ARGUMENTS:

In this viewpoint, author Alan D. Abbey poses ethical questions concerning balance and fairness in journalism. Should media entities be obligated to be balanced and show opposing perspectives? Why or why not?

Chapter 2

What Constitutes Fake News?

Consumers are finding it increasingly difficult to determine what is real.

Viewpoint 1

There Is a Difference Between Fake News and Unverified News

"Fake news is what the Onion produces. And much of it is very clever."

a1skeptic

In the following viewpoint, an anonymous blogger writing under the pseudonym "a1skeptic" argues the definition of "fake news" by discussing the report released by Buzzfeed prior to the 2017 inauguration of President Donald J. Trump. Buzzfeed's report initially seemed damning to Trump. It was ultimately revealed to be full of information that is difficult to verify, however, which makes it "unverified" or "unverifiable" and a product of poor journalism. While also strongly expressing his or her own political views, the author also goes on to discuss how the distinction between fake news and unverified news can be unclear.

"The Difference Between Fake News and Unverified News," a1skeptic, January 12, 2017. Reprinted by permission.

1. Did Buzzfeed verify the allegation about the Trump dossier before publishing its story?

2. Who was briefed on the dossier?

3. What source does the author cite as an obvious example of fake news?

As some of you know, the Donald, Herr Obergropenführer, President-elect Kumquat, was attacked the other day through Buzzfeed, which published an article claiming that "a dossier, compiled by a person who has claimed to be a former British intelligence official, alleges Russia has compromising information on Trump."

As Buzzfeed itself acknowledged, the "allegations are unverified," and the "report contains errors."

So, this is unverified news.

It was, however, credible enough that the intelligence services of the United States thought it necessary to brief both the outgoing President (Obama) and the incoming President (Kumquat). As well as the top eight leaders of the House and the Senate.

CNN found out about the briefing and thought that was newsworthy enough to go with it.

The Donald, in his restrained way, immediately branded the allegations as "FAKE NEWS," demonstrating that he does not grasp the difference between the definitions of "fake" and "unverified."

Fake news is what the Onion produces. And much of it is very clever. Or it's things like the allegations that Hillary Clinton's campaign was running a child prostitution ring out of a pizza parlor in Washington D.C., leading some loony-tune to storm the parlor and almost kill someone. Or that Hillary was involved in a conspiracy to murder Vince Foster. That's fake news.

This is not.

As reported by BuzzFeed, the allegations are, among other things, that there is a dossier, *"which is a collection of memos written over a period of months, includes specific, unverified, and potentially*

The proliferation of sketchy reporting, unverified information, and fake news can make us question the value of the news we get altogether.

unverifiable allegations of contact between Trump aides and Russian operatives, and graphic claims of sexual acts documented by the Russians. The document was prepared for political opponents of Trump by a person who is understood to be a former British intelligence agent."

The document itself has been uploaded to documentcloud.org. It's titled "Company Intelligence Report 2016/080," and makes among other things, the following allegations:

1. That the Russian regime has been cultivating, supporting and assisting Trump for at least 5 years. The aim, endorsed by Putin, has been to encourage divisions in western alliance.
2. That so far TRUMP has declined various sweetener real estate business deals offered him in Russia in order to further the Kremlin's cultivation of him.

3. That Trump and his inner circle have, however, accepted a regular flow of intelligence from the Kremlin, including on his Democratic and other political rivals.

4. That a former top Russian intelligence officer claims FSB has compromised Trump through his activities in Moscow sufficiently to be able to blackmail him. According to several knowledgeable sources, his conduct in Moscow has included perverted sexual acts which have been arranged and monitored by the FSB.

5. That a dossier of compromising material on Hillary Clinton had also been collated by the Russian Intelligence Services over many years and mainly comprised bugged conversations she had on various visits to Russia and intercepted phone calls, but that there was no embarrassing conduct.

Needless to say, this kind of information is very hard to verify. You can't just call up the Russian secret service and ask them whether they have the good on the Obergropenführer. I don't know that any of this is true, but the schadenfreude part of me so wants this to be true. I mean, c'mon my friends: you all KNOW that the Russians didn't just hack into the DNC, you know that they hacked into the RNC as well. And you KNOW that the Russians have Trump's tax returns. Somebody sure does. And you KNOW that Putin is many steps ahead of Trump—like a chessman playing checkers—and while he may not have known that Trump would run for President, he knew that Trump was a big deal in the United States.

Can you imagine if we get some nice juicy Trump sex tapes at the beginning of his Presidency. Then Kellyanne Conway can give more pathetic interviews about how the Democrats and the left are trying to "delegitimize" the Trump Presidency.

Oh, please let it be true!

Unpatriotic of me? Not at all. Trump is the guy who's been defending Putin all along. And the most patriotic thing that I could wish for is that the Trump Presidency goes up in flames—so richly deserved—and that we make America SAFE again.

Because right now it is not safe.

EVALUATING THE AUTHOR'S ARGUMENTS:

In this viewpoint, the anonymous author writing under the pseudonym "a1skeptic" discusses the difference in definitions between "unverified news" and "fake news." Does the author's definition do enough to create a distinction? How is a layperson supposed to determine what is accurate and what is fake? Do the author's anonymity and tone discredit him or her?

Viewpoint 2

Comments on News Stories Are Rarely Beneficial

"Those commenting on the news tend to be male, have lower levels of education, and have lower incomes."

Shan Wang

In the following viewpoint, Shan Wang questions who posts comments on news stories and why they do it. Wang also points out that those who choose to comment heavily prefer to have more interaction with the writer of the story being commented on, but would not be willing to pay to do so. Wang is a staff writer at the Nieman Lab. She previously worked for Harvard University Press and has reported for Boston.com and the New England Center for Investigative Reporting.

AS YOU READ, CONSIDER THE FOLLOWING QUESTIONS:

1. What percentage of Americans have posted a comment in response to a news story?

2. What top resason did respondents give for leaving comments?

3. What percentage of respondents believe offensive comments should be removed?

"Who Is Posting Comments on News Stories, and Why Do They Do It?" by Shan Wang, the President and Fellows of Harvard College, March 14, 2016. Reprinted by permission. Published by agreement with the Nieman Foundation for Journalism.

Who's actually adding to the civil discourse/garbage fire that is the comments section of news sites (the sites that still keep open a place for such reader contributions, at least)? Fifty-five percent of Americans have posted an online comment and 78 percent have read comments, according to a report released Monday at SXSW by the Engaging News Project out of the University of Texas at Austin. The report also suggests, however, that over half of Americans have never read news-related comments or commented anywhere (dedicated apps, social media, the news sites themselves) about the news. Fourteen percent have never left any sort of comments on news stories.

Of those leaving news comments, the majority posted via social media (77.9 percent), and most (53 percent) posted on a monthly basis or even less frequently.

The report pulls out a few other findings about the demographics of news commenters:

- Compared to those who read news comments but did not themselves comment, those commenting on the news "tend[ed] to be more male, have lower levels of education, and have lower incomes."
- Compared to those who posted comments on the news infrequently, those who posted comments on the news on a weekly basis (or even more frequently) were similarly "more male, have lower levels of education, and have lower incomes. They [were] less white and more Hispanic."

Respondents were asked why they left comments. Responses ran the gamut, but the top reason was "to express an emotion or an opinion," followed by "adding information," "correcting inaccuracies or misinformation," and "taking part in the debate." These responses varied based on the topic people commented on most frequently:

FAST FACT

Twitter users are more likely to retweet news than to write an original post about the news.

- Those who commented most on U.S. politics did so to express an emotion or opinion,

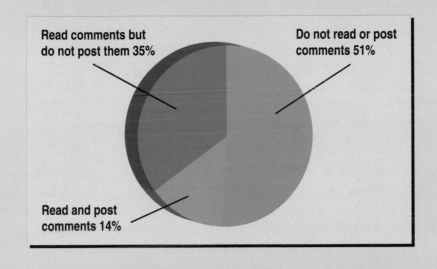

Americans and Reader Comments About the News

Read comments but do not post them 35%

Do not read or post comments 51%

Read and post comments 14%

Source: The Engaging News Project

to take part in the debate, to educate others, and to balance the discussion, compared to those who commented most on stories about their neighborhood or community.

- Those who commented most frequently on news about their neighborhood or community were more likely to comment to share an experience, be part of the community, or show sympathy to others, compared to those who commented most on U.S. politics.

Not surprisingly, the report also found that those who avoided commenting on the news or avoided reading comments on the news felt that comment sections were uncivil and argumentative. But when it came to policing comment sections, the report found an even split between people who believed news organizations should remove offensive comments (42 percent) and those who believed comments constitute free speech (41.6 percent).

The responses to the survey were collected between November and December 2015 by market research group GfK from a "representative

"Pizzagate," a false story about a child sex ring connected to the Comet pizza parlor and Hillary Clinton's campaign manager, compelled one would-be vigilante to investigate and open fire in the restaurant.

sample" of Americans, with complete data from 1,471 respondents. The report breaks out a number of other tidbits around online news commenting, including whether commenters would like journalists/experts to weigh in on facts (yes) and whether they'd be willing to pay for comments (no).

EVALUATING THE AUTHOR'S ARGUMENTS:

Viewpoint author Shan Wang breaks down the demographics of people who post comments to online stories. Consider whether those who do read and post in comments sections are more informed and/or educated than those who avoid adding commentary to comments sections.

Everyone Should Learn How to Spot Fake News

"It's easy to figure out what's real and what's imaginary if you're armed with some critical thinking and fact-checking tools of the trade."

Eugene Kiely and Lori Robertson

In the following viewpoint, Eugene Kiely and Lori Robertson discuss fake news and how a reader can think critically when presented with a piece that is potentially maliciously fictitious. The authors also discuss what fake news purveyors do to make their websites look like credible news websites. Additionally, the authors discuss the importance of having readers understand their own biases when reading and analyzing inflammatory news stories that may or may not be factual. Kiely is director of FactCheck.org. Robertson is managing editor of FactCheck.org

AS YOU READ, CONSIDER THE FOLLOWING QUESTIONS:

1. What website is a key resource for exposing false viral claims?

2. How do the authors suggest treating headlines?

3. How can checking an article's date tell a reader that a story is fake?

"How to Spot Fake News," by Eugene Kiely and Lori Robertson, FactCheck.org, a project of the Annenberg Public Policy Center, November 18, 2016. Reprinted by permission.

Fake news is nothing new. But bogus stories can reach more people more quickly via social media than what good old-fashioned viral emails could accomplish in years past.

Concern about the phenomenon led Facebook and Google to announce that they'll crack down on fake news sites, restricting their ability to garner ad revenue. Perhaps that could dissipate the amount of malarkey online, though news consumers themselves are the best defense against the spread of misinformation.

Not all of the misinformation being passed along online is complete fiction, though some of it is. Snopes.com has been exposing false viral claims since the mid 1990s, whether that's fabricated messages, distortions containing bits of truth and everything in between. Founder David Mikkelson warned in a Nov. 17 article not to lump everything into the "fake news" category. "The fictions and fabrications that comprise fake news are but a subset of the larger *bad news* phenomenon, which also encompasses many forms of shoddy, unresearched, error-filled, and deliberately misleading reporting that do a disservice to everyone," he wrote.

A lot of these viral claims aren't "news" at all, but fiction, satire and efforts to fool readers into thinking they're for real.

We've long encouraged readers to be skeptical of viral claims, and make good use of the delete key when a chain email hits their inboxes. In December 2007, we launched our Ask FactCheck feature, where we answer readers' questions, the vast majority of which concern viral emails, social media memes and the like. Our first story was about a made-up email that claimed then-House Speaker Nancy Pelosi wanted to put a "windfall" tax on all stock profits of 100 percent and give the money to, the email claimed, "the 12 Million Illegal Immigrants and other unemployed minorities." We called it "a malicious fabrication"—that's "fake news" in today's parlance.

In 2008, we tried to get readers to rid their inboxes of this kind of garbage. We described a list of red flags—we called them Key Characteristics of Bogusness—that were clear tip-offs that a chain email wasn't legitimate. Among them: an anonymous author; excessive exclamation points, capital letters and misspellings; entreaties that "This is NOT a hoax!"; and links to sourcing that does not support or completely contradicts the claims being made.

TheOnion The Onion
Congress Takes Group Of Schoolchildren Hostage
onion.com/r1pM9h #CongressHostage
6 hours ago

TheOnion The Onion
BREAKING: Capitol building being evacuated. 12 children held
hostage by group of armed congressmen. #CongressHostage
6 hours ago

TheOnion The Onion
BREAKING: Witnesses reporting screams and gunfire heard
inside Capitol building.
6 hours ago ☆ Favorite ⇄ Retweet ↰ Reply

The Onion is an obviously satirical news source, but the legitimacy of many other organizations can be trickier to discern.

Those all still hold true, but fake stories—as in, completely made-up "news"—has grown more sophisticated, often presented on a site designed to look (sort of) like a legitimate news organization. Still, we find it's easy to figure out what's real and what's imaginary if you're armed with some critical thinking and fact-checking tools of the trade.

Here's our advice on how to spot a fake:

Consider the Source

In recent months, we've fact-checked fake news from abcnews.com.co (not the actual URL for ABC News), WTOE 5 News (whose "about" page says it's "a fantasy news website"), and the Boston Tribune (whose "contact us" page lists only a gmail address). Earlier this year, we debunked the claim that the Obamas were buying a vacation home in Dubai, a made-up missive that came from WhatDoesItMean.com, which describes itself as "One Of The Top Ranked Websites In The World for New World Order, Conspiracy Theories and Alternative News" and further says on its site that most of what it publishes is fiction.

Clearly, some of these sites do provide a "fantasy news" or sat-ire warning, like WTOE 5, which published the bogus headline,

"Pope Francis Shocks World, Endorses Donald Trump for President, Releases Statement." Others aren't so upfront, like the Boston Tribune, which doesn't provide any information on its mission, staff members or physical location—further signs that maybe this site isn't a legitimate news organization. The site, in fact, changed its name from Associated Media Coverage, after its work had been debunked by fact-checking organizations.

Snopes.com, which has been writing about viral claims and online rumors since the mid-1990s, maintains a list of known fake news websites, several of which have emerged in the past two years.

Read Beyond the Headline

If a provocative headline drew your attention, read a little further before you decide to pass along the shocking information. Even in legitimate news stories, the headline doesn't always tell the whole story. But fake news, particularly efforts to be satirical, can include several revealing signs in the text. That abcnews.com.co story that we checked, headlined "Obama Signs Executive Order Banning The Pledge Of Allegiance In Schools Nationwide," went on to quote "Fappy the Anti-Masturbation Dolphin." We have to assume that the many readers who asked us whether this viral rumor was true hadn't read the full story.

Check the Author

Another tell-tale sign of a fake story is often the byline. The pledge of allegiance story on abcnews.com.co was supposedly written by "Jimmy Rustling." Who is he? Well, his author page claims he is a "doctor" who won "fourteen Peabody awards and a handful of Pulitzer Prizes." Pretty impressive, if true. But it's not. No one by the name of "Rustling" has won a Pulitzer or Peabody award. The photo accompanying Rustling's bio is also displayed on another bogus story on a different site, but this time under the byline "Darius Rubics." The Dubai story was written by "Sorcha Faal, and as reported to her Western Subscribers." The Pope Francis story has no byline at all.

What's the Support?

Many times these bogus stories will cite official—or official-sounding—sources, but once you look into it, the source doesn't back up the claim. For instance, the Boston Tribune site wrongly claimed that President Obama's mother-in-law was going to get a lifetime government pension for having babysat her granddaughters in the White House, citing "the Civil Service Retirement Act" and providing a link. But the link to a government benefits website doesn't support the claim at all.

The banning-the-pledge story cites the number of an actual executive order—you can look it up. It doesn't have anything to do with the Pledge of Allegiance.

Another viral claim we checked a year ago was a graphic purporting to show crime statistics on the percentage of whites killed by blacks and other murder statistics by race. Then-presidential candidate Donald Trump retweeted it, telling Fox News commentator Bill O'Reilly that it came "from sources that are very credible." But almost every figure in the image was wrong—FBI crime data is publicly available—and the supposed source given for the data, "Crime Statistics Bureau–San Francisco," doesn't exist.

Recently, we've received several questions about a fake news story on the admittedly satirical site Nevada County Scooper, which wrote that Vice President-elect Mike Pence, in a "surprise announcement," credited gay conversion therapy for saving his marriage. Clearly such a "surprise announcement" would garner media coverage beyond a website you've never heard of. In fact, if you Google this, the first link that comes up is a Snopes.com article revealing that this is fake news.

Check the Date

Some false stories aren't completely fake, but rather distortions of real events. These mendacious claims can take a legitimate news story and twist what it says—or even claim that something that happened long ago is related to current events.

Since Trump was elected president, we've received many inquiries from readers wanting to know whether Ford had moved car production from Mexico to Ohio, because of Trump's election. Readers cited various blog items that quoted from and linked to a CNN Money article titled "Ford shifts truck production from Mexico to Ohio." But that story is from August 2015, clearly not evidence of Ford making any move due to the outcome of the election. (A reminder again to check the support for these claims.)

One deceptive website didn't credit CNN, but instead took CNN's 2015 story and slapped a new headline and publication date on it, claiming, "Since Donald Trump Won The Presidency... Ford Shifts Truck Production From Mexico To Ohio." Not only is that a bogus headline, but the deception involves copyright infringement.

If this Ford story sounds familiar, that's because the CNN article has been distorted before.

In October 2015, Trump wrongly boasted that Ford had changed its plans to build new plants in Mexico, and instead would build a plant in Ohio. Trump took credit for Ford's alleged change of heart and tweeted a link to a story on a blog called Prntly.com, which cited the CNN Money story. But Ford hadn't changed its plans at all, and Trump deserved no credit.

In fact, the CNN article was about the transfer of some pickup assembly work from Mexico to Ohio, a move that was announced by Ford in March 2014. The plans for new plants in Mexico were still on, Ford said. "Ford has not spoken with Mr. Trump, nor have we made any changes to our plans," Ford said in a statement.

Is This Some Kind of Joke?

Remember, there is such thing as satire. Normally, it's clearly labeled as such, and sometimes it's even funny. Andy Borowitz has been writing a satirical news column, the Borowitz Report, since 2001, and it has appeared in the *New Yorker* since 2012. But not everyone gets the jokes. We've fielded several questions on whether Borowitz's work is true.

Among the headlines our readers have flagged: "Putin Appears with Trump in Flurry of Swing-State Rallies" and "Trump Threatens to Skip Remaining Debates If Hillary Is There." When we told readers these were satirical columns, some indicated that they suspected the details were far-fetched but wanted to be sure.

FAST FACT

California is proposing that lessons be added to the school curriculum teaching how to tell real news from fake news.

And then there's the more debatable forms of satire, designed to pull one over on the reader. That "Fappy the Anti-Masturbation Dolphin" story? That's the work of online hoaxer Paul Horner, whose "greatest coup," as described by the *Washington Post* in 2014, was when Fox News mentioned, as fact, a fake piece titled, "Obama uses own money to open Muslim museum amid government shutdown." Horner told the *Post* after the election that he was concerned his hoaxes aimed at Trump supporters may have helped the campaign.

The posts by Horner and others—whether termed satire or simply "fake news"—are designed to encourage clicks, and generate money for the creator through ad revenue. Horner told the *Washington Post* he makes a living off his posts. Asked why his material gets so many views, Horner responded, "They just keep passing stuff around. Nobody fact-checks anything anymore."

Check Your Biases

We know this is difficult. Confirmation bias leads people to put more stock in information that confirms their beliefs and discount information that doesn't. But the next time you're automatically appalled at some Facebook post concerning, say, a politician you oppose, take a moment to check it out.

Try this simple test: What other stories have been posted to the "news" website that is the source of the story that just popped up in your Facebook feed? You may be predisposed to believe that Obama bought a house in Dubai, but how about a story on the same site that carries this headline: "Antarctica 'Guardians' Retaliate Against America With Massive New Zealand Earthquake." That, too, was written by the prolific "Sorcha Faal, and as reported to her Western Subscribers."

We're encouraged by some of the responses we get from readers, who—like the ones uncertain of Borowitz's columns—express doubt in the outrageous, and just want to be sure their skepticism is justified. But we are equally discouraged when we see debunked claims gain new life.

We've seen the resurgence of a fake quote from Donald Trump since the election—a viral image that circulated last year claims Trump told *People* magazine in 1998: "If I were to run, I'd run as a Republican. They're the dumbest group of voters in the country. They believe anything on Fox News. I could lie and they'd still eat it up. I bet my numbers would be terrific." We found no such quote in *People*'s archives from 1998, or any other year. And a public relations representative for the magazine confirmed that. *People*'s Julie Farin told us in an email last year: "We combed through every Trump story in our archive. We couldn't find anything remotely like this quote—and no interview at all in 1998."

Comedian Amy Schumer may have contributed to the revival of this fake meme. She put it on Instagram, adding at the end of a lengthy message, "Yes this quote is fake but it doesn't matter."

Consult the Experts

We know you're busy, and some of this debunking takes time. But we get paid to do this kind of work. Between FactCheck.org, Snopes.com, the *Washington Post* Fact Checker and PolitiFact.com, it's likely at least one has already fact-checked the latest viral claim to pop up in your news feed.

FactCheck.org was among a network of independent fact-checkers who signed an open letter to Facebook's Mark Zuckerberg suggesting that Facebook "start an open conversation on the principles that could underpin a more accurate news ecosystem on its News Feed." We hope that conversation happens, but news readers themselves remain the first line of defense against fake news.

On our Viral Spiral page, we list some of the claims we get asked about the most. And if you encounter a new claim you'd like us to investigate, email us at editor@factcheck.org.

EVALUATING THE AUTHORS' ARGUMENTS:

The authors of this viewpoint discuss the ways a reader can identify fake news websites that seem legitimate. In late 2016, Google and Facebook announced their plan to take down fake news sites by restricting their ability to garner ad revenue, but with the amount of fake news being posted to social media sites, is that enough? Why or why not?

Viewpoint 4

Television Is Still the Preferred Source for News

Krysten Crawford

"Both the advent of cheap newsprint and television were considered dangerous to American democracy."

In the following viewpoint, Krysten Crawford discusses a Stanford University study that examined fake news and its effects on the 2016 US presidential election. The study, authored by economists Matthew Gentzkow and Hunt Allcott, determined that social media was not the dominant news source in the run-up to the election. Instead, television remained the go-to source for political news. This study does not conclude one way or the other if fake news swayed the election but does indicate that it was not as influential as perceived. Crawford is a Bay Area journalist.

AS YOU READ, CONSIDER THE FOLLOWING QUESTIONS:

1. According to the study, what percentage of Americans primarily relied on social media sites for election coverage?

2. Can social media become more hazardous to future elections, according to the viewpoint?

3. How many people were featured in the post-election online survey?

"Stanford Study Examines Fake News and the 2016 Presidential Election," by Krysten Crawford, Stanford University, January 18, 2017. Reprinted by permission.

Of all the heated debates surrounding the 2016 presidential race, the controversy over so-called "fake news" and its potential impact on Donald Trump's victory has been among the fiercest.

Now there's concrete data proposing that false news stories may not have been as persuasive and influential as is often suggested. But the economists behind the research do not conclude one way or the other whether fake news swayed the election.

On Wednesday, economists Matthew Gentzkow of Stanford and Hunt Allcott of New York University released a study also showing that social media played a much smaller role in the election than some might think.

"A reader of our study could very reasonably say, based on our set of facts, that it is unlikely that fake news swayed the election," said Gentzkow, an economics professor and senior fellow at the Stanford Institute for Economic Policy Research (SIEPR).

"But that conclusion ultimately depends on what readers think is a reasonable benchmark for the persuasiveness of an individual fake news story," he said.

The timing of the working paper, "Social Media and Fake News in the 2016 Election," is critical. Trump's victory has been dogged by claims that false news stories—including false reports that Hillary Clinton sold weapons to ISIS and the pope had endorsed Trump— altered the outcome.

Facebook and other social media sites have also come under attack for allowing fabricated news stories to circulate unchecked on their platforms.

"There are lots of pieces to this puzzle," said Gentzkow, referring to the impact of social media on the election.

Social Media: "Important, but Not Dominant"

In their study, Gentzkow and Allcott analyzed three sets of data. The first tracked the amount of traffic on news websites that was directed by social media. The second examined the top fake news stories identified by BuzzFeed and two prominent fact-checking sites, Snopes and PolitiFact. The third consisted of the researchers' own post-election online survey of 1,200 voters.

Gentzkow and Allcott show that social media wasn't the major source of political news for most Americans in 2016; only 14 percent say they relied on Facebook and other social media sites as their most important source of election coverage.

"Social media was an important but not dominant source of news in the run-up to the election," the authors write. Television, it turns out, remains the go-to place for political news.

In the three months before the election, pro-Trump fabricated stories tracked by the researchers were shared a total of 30 million times, nearly quadruple the number of pro-Clinton shares. Even so, Gentzkow and Allcott find that the most widely circulated hoaxes were seen by only a small fraction of Americans. And only about half of those who saw a false news story believed it.

Even if a voter recalled a fake news story and believed what it said, the story would need to have been surprisingly persuasive to have changed his or her vote.

"For fake news to have changed the outcome of the election, a single fake news story would need to have convinced about 0.7 percent of Clinton voters and non-voters who saw it to shift their votes to Trump, a persuasion rate equivalent to seeing 36 television campaign ads," the authors conclude.

The study comes with important caveats. Gentzkow said, for example, that a voter doesn't necessarily need to recall a specific news story in order to have developed a negative view of either Trump or Clinton.

A Deeper Partisan Divide?

The 2016 election isn't the only time when technology has been seen as a threat to electoral politics, Gentzkow and Allcott note. Both the advent of cheap newsprint and television were considered dangerous to American democracy.

Stories circulating on social media—both factual and ficticious—turned out to have a significant effect on the result of the 2016 presidential election.

Social media is creating its own set of hazards with potentially profound implications, Gentzkow said. Increasingly, the influence of major media outlets is diminishing, especially at a time when anyone can dream up and disseminate a story, real or not, with nothing more than an imagination and Internet access.

Factor in the possibility that social media could further segregate voters based on party affiliation and "you have a potential game-changer in terms of the degree of polarization in this country," Gentzkow said.

EVALUATING THE AUTHOR'S ARGUMENTS:

Viewpoint author Krysten Crawford points out that the advents of both cheap newsprint and television were also once considered dangerous to American democracy. Will social media follow that same pattern? Why or why not?

Chapter 3

How Can We Fight Fake News?

Internet news is here to stay, so we must become smarter consumers.

Viewpoint

1

The Fight Against Fake News Will Be Ongoing

"The public has a positive view of fact-checking, although Republicans, as well as people who are less informed, educated and politically knowledgeable, view the format less favorably."

Elia Powers

In the following viewpoint, Elia Powers discusses the facts behind the dissemination of fake news and the importance of fact-checking, which can change the beliefs of the misinformed. Powers contends that fact-checking generally helps people become better informed about issues under discussion. Conversely, Powers points out that political professionals anticipate fact-checking and regularly ignore fact-checks that go against their core message. It is now the onus of media outlets to rebuild trust with its readers by engaging more, becoming more transparent, and involving readers in the newsgathering process. Powers is an assistant professor of journalism and new media at Towson University. He writes regularly about news literacy, audience engagement, and non-profit journalism.

1. What was the top concern among recent journalism graduates about the future of journalism?

2. How does the author suggest that trust in the news media can be rebuilt?

3. Why does one expert believe news literacy training programs are limited in solving the problem?

More than five years ago, Tom Rosenstiel and Bill Kovach released their guide to helping news consumers sort fact from fiction. "Blur: How to Know What's True in the Age of Information Overload" covers many topics—how to evaluate sources, how to know whether a news account is complete, how to verify questionable claims—that are timely given the avalanche of information that circulated during this election year.

One line in the first chapter is particularly prescient given the recent influx of fake news (wholly false stories) and misinformation (false or inaccurate information): "Citizens have more voice, but those who would manipulate the public for political gain or profit—be it corporations or the government—have more direct access to the public as well."

Rosenstiel could never have predicted the details of how this would soon play out: teenagers in Macedonia, among others, profiting off fake news they created about the 2016 presidential election that spread quickly through social media. How would he amend his book given all that's happened in the last year?

"The problems of misinformation, rumor and confirmation bias were not created by a team in Russia and Macedonia," Rosenstiel said in an interview. "They were exploited by a team in Russia and Macedonia."

"Fake news isn't like a leaky pipe where you tighten it with a proper seal and then it's fixed for 20 years," Rosenstiel added. "Fake news and the problem it represents are more like crime and you are a police force. You can police it better or worse, but you are fighting it perpetually. You need better techniques and better technology to do it."

Plenty of people are responding with technological solutions and lists of false and misleading news sources. Rosenstiel, a longtime journalist and press critic, founder of the Pew Research Center's Project for Excellence in Journalism, and executive director of the American Press Institute, isn't in the business of creating new technology. But he has plenty of thoughts about techniques journalists and journalism educators can use to combat fake news and misinformation, and provide appealing alternatives for news consumers.

His thinking is informed by not only his professional experiences but research sponsored by API that examined the effectiveness of fact-checking and how to improve its practice in newsrooms. Funded by the Rita Allen Foundation, the William and Flora Hewlett Foundation and the Democracy Fund, the studies were part of the Fact-Checking Project, aimed to improve and expand political and accountability journalism in the run-up to the 2016 presidential election.

Part one of this series examined how foundations spent recent years investing in such projects, as well as public-interest journalism and news literacy education, in an effort to promote factual journalism that competes with misinformation and fake news. After a campaign that was filled with plenty of falsehoods, many are wondering what comes next for journalism and journalism educators. Part two takes up this question by looking at recent research, and asking those involved in the projects what they have learned and what may come next.

Just the Facts

When API surveyed more than 10,000 journalism and communication graduates last year about what they viewed as the biggest challenges facing journalism, the most common answer wasn't the economic model of news or the public's interest in quality journalism. It was, by a sizable margin, opinion and false information on the internet.

"That answer surprised me," Rosenstiel said. "That's a very strong response—there's just too much junk out there."

News literacy programs are teaching students to be smarter consumers of news.

Research from API's Fact-Checking Project, all completed before the 2016 presidential campaign began in earnest, provided plenty of grist for supporters of fact-checking. Among the findings

- Fact-checking coverage greatly increased during the 2012 campaign, with the growth mostly concentrated in newsrooms with dedicated fact-checkers. Findings suggest that efforts to create or extend dedicated fact-checking operations and to train reporters are the most effective ways of growing the practice.
- The public has a positive view of fact-checking, although Republicans, as well as people who are less informed, educated and politically knowledgeable, view the format less favorably. Fact-checks generally help people become better informed and knowledgeable about the issues under discussion.
- Readers prefer fact-checking that uses a graphical meter or truth scale (think pants on fire or Pinocchio) along with a written analysis of claims, rather than just latter. Both approaches proved equally effective in challenging political misinformation.
- Fact-checking—even a single correction—can substantially reduce misperceptions, even in the long-term.
- Tweets correcting falsehoods or retweets of those corrections are "completely swamped by the tweets making or repeating the claim," although the amount of misinformation decreases over time. Sentiment toward fact-checking on Twitter is largely positive, and the targets of fact-checking are seen in a mostly negative light.
- Political professionals anticipate fact-checking and regularly "weaponize" fact checks by citing them in advertisements and campaign material to undermine their opponents' credibility and refute attacks. They ignore fact-checks that go against their core message, and sometimes attack the fact-checkers.

Other research co-authored by Brendan Nyhan, a Dartmouth College political scientist who co-authored several of the API project studies, revealed mixed results. Studies found that correcting people's false beliefs can be ineffective or lead them to hold onto their views even more strongly. But other research suggested that fact-checking can be effective.

Nyhan's most recent co-authored study, which he wrote about in the *New York Times* just before Election Day, found that correcting Donald Trump's false claim that the national crime rate is rising reduced the prevalence of people's false beliefs. The study found partial evidence that questioning the validity of the correction undermined its effects on Trump supporters. Results prompted Nyhan to conclude that "Despite all the hand-wringing, we do not seem to have entered a post-truth era."

Post-election, Nyhan argued that journalists should not give up on fact-checking Trump's false claims but should be careful not to play into his hands. "These stories have to de-emphasize the claim itself, emphasize the news value of the president-elect being so widely irresponsible," he told *ProPublica*.

Rosenstiel said he remains confident in the importance and effi-cacy of fact-checking.

"I think the notion of a post-fact or post-truth world is a gross misunderstanding of what happened," Rosenstiel said. "The point of fact-checking is not to determine who lied less but to inform voters of whether or not and where political actors are stretching the truth."

Elizabeth Good Christopherson, president and CEO of the Rita Allen Foundation (one of the API research co-funders), said in an e-mail that "despite talk of this being the 'post-truth' election, there are also signs that fact-checking is driving audience engagement."

Still, there is much left to research. "The election showed that there is still a lot we don't know about how and when facts matter," Christopherson said.

Building Trust Through Community Engagement, Transparency

By many measures, trust in the news media is at a record low. Focusing on getting facts right is critical to rebuilding that trust, according to a study released earlier this year by the Media Insight Project, an initia-tive of API and the Associated Press-NORC Center for Public Affairs Research. Respondents rated accuracy as the most important general principle related to trust.

The vast majority also said news outlet transparency—whether "I know and trust its journalists" and "it explains the way it gathers and reports news and information"—was an important trust principle.

"The election has foregrounded this question of a lack of trust," said Tom Glaisyer, chair of the Democracy Fund's public square program. "The lack of a newsroom-community connection, i.e. a lack of trust in news, has to be rebuilt."

Glaisyer points to News Voices: New Jersey, a project it co-funds, as one promising model. The pilot program aims to build interest and engagement in local news by holding forums for journalists, activists and other New Jersey residents to discuss—and potentially collaborate on—issues of local concern.

Jennifer Preston, vice president of journalism at the John S. and James L. Knight Foundation, said such initiatives are important.

"We have a tremendous opportunity to use this challenging moment to rebuild trust," she said. "Journalists and journalism need to do a better job listening to our communities, to engage more deeply with the people we cover, bring them into the newsgathering process and involve them in our reporting,"

One way journalists can give readers a window into the news-gathering process, Rosenstiel said, is to increase transparency and documentation. Writing for Brookings Institution, he argued that the presentation of reportorial news needs to change. "The atomic unit of news in the past was the 'news story,' the lovely narrative, beautifully written… The new atomic unit of news must actually be the report-ing—what the story learned—and the proof that establishes it. News people must now adopt forms, templates, and structures that make that proof—the evidence—become more explicit."

He envisions a prominently displayed box that presents questions such as "What is new about this story? What is the evidence? Who are the sources? What proof do they offer? What is still missing or unknown?"

"It will raise the bar for the verification that people put into their reporting," Rosenstiel said in an interview. "If they have to lay these things bare and answer questions for readers that a skeptical editor would ask, that will make the reporting stronger."

Increased transparency, coupled with clearer labeling of what's news, opinion and news analysis, will also help readers become more discerning, Rosenstiel said.

"You've taken news literacy and you've put it out into the public," he said. "You are training readers to ask these questions. The curric-ulum is potentially embedded in the technology. I actually think you can teach news literacy potentially at scale by building the stories differently."

Scaling Up News Literacy Education

How to teach news literacy at scale is the subject of recent research conducted by the Center for Information & Research on Civic Learning and Engagement at Tufts University with financial support from the Democracy Fund.

Abby Kiesa, director of impact at CIRCLE, said in an interview that "a constellation of approaches to teaching news literacy are needed to reach different types of young people in different locations and with different identities."

The most high-profile of those approaches are news literacy training in schools, primarily done through the News Literacy Project and the Center for News Literacy at Stony Brook University. The News Literacy Project, targeting middle and high school students, does classroom, after-school and e-learning training, in addition to professional development for teachers. Its virtual classroom program is intended to broaden the project's reach. The Center for News Literacy, historically focused on higher education, has taught news literacy to thousands of students at Stony Brook and provided free training and materials to educators at dozens of universities. More recently, it has broadened its reach by developing curriculum materials for high schools and the general public through a digital resource center. Next month the center is sponsoring a massive open online course, "Making Sense of the News: News Literacy Lessons for Digital Citizens," through Coursera.

FAST FACT

The biggest challenges facing journalism, according to recent graduates of the discipline, is the presence of false information on the internet.

Glaisyer, the Democracy Fund's public square program director, said classroom-based news literacy education is important but has limitations in its scope.

Added Larry Kramer, president of the Hewlett Foundation, which makes education grants: "Civic education and media literacy are good as far as they go, but they just don't go very far. This is a mass society problem."

Kiesa said she considered this concern in her research. "Beyond schools, where are the other places where people are implicitly learning things?" she said.

Her proposal for broadening the reach of news literacy education includes targeting after-school programs, youth organizing groups and youth media organizations. Jessica Clark, director of research and strategy at Media Impact Funders, said news literacy education could be weaved into agricultural extension programs or public broadcasting stations in rural communities in order to reach areas with less access to existing training.

Another idea, similar to Rosenstiel's, is to "explore what publishers and tech companies can do to explicitly or implicitly teach skills through what they are doing," Kiesa said. News outlets and fact-checking groups have already contributed tipsheets on how to spot fake news.

These disparate ideas share common goals: Increase demand for trustworthy information and train news consumers to be skeptical about what they see online.

"You have to build a strong public will to take responsibility for consuming credible news," Kramer said. "You're never going to be able to control the flow of information."

EVALUATING THE AUTHOR'S ARGUMENTS:

Viewpoint author Elia Powers points out that many researchers do not believe that we live in a "post-truth" era and that journalists should continue to fact-check false claims, primarily by de-emphasizing the claim itself. Why is de-emphasizing the false claim an important aspect of fact-checking?

Technology Can Help When Critical Thinking Fails

Victoria L. Rubin, Yimin Chen, and Niall J. Conroy

"In the race to capture eyeballs, being first and flashy is better than being accurate."

In the following viewpoint, Victoria L. Rubin, Yimin Chen, and Niall J. Conroy argue that technology can be used to fight fake news by becoming another level of quality, unbiased fact-checking when our own internal critical thinking skills fail us. The authors discuss uses of "deception detection" and "satirical news detection" algorithms to separate fake, unverified, satirical, or otherwise inaccurate news from legitimate stories. Rubin, Chen, and Conroy are with the faculty of information and media studies at the University of Western Ontario.

AS YOU READ, CONSIDER THE FOLLOWING QUESTIONS:

1. According to the viewpoint, how much annual revenue is in digital ads?

2. What percentage of American adults get some of their news from Facebook?

3. What percentage of "deception detection" in news does the author consider successful?

"Education and Automation: Tools for Navigating a Sea of Fake News," by Victoria L. Rubin, Yimin Chen, and Niall J. Conroy, This article first appeared at Undark.org, November 23, 2016. Reprinted by permission.

Newsrooms around the world have been quietly whispering about the slow death of journalism for decades, but 2016 has seen that rumbling become a roar. Spurred on in no small part by one of the most-watched and most controversial presidential races in recent U.S. history, the manufacture of perilous misinformation, distributed *en masse*, has bred an increasingly toxic online news environment.

The Oxford English Dictionary has named "post-truth" as its word of the year, referring to the circumstance "in which objective facts are less influential in shaping public opinion than appeals to emotion and personal belief." That might be going too far, but there is no doubt that the internet has changed the way that news is created and consumed. Speed and spectacle are incentivized in reporting, at the cost of fact-checking and verification.

What's at Stake

In a media economy based on clicks and views, each hit on a web page translates directly to dollars—annual digital ad spending grew to $59.6 billion in the U.S. in the past year. On the other hand, the value of responsible reporting is extremely hard to quantify. Compounding the problem, news aggregators and social media sites have further eroded the value on institutional reputation by decontextualizing news from its source. In the race to capture eyeballs, being first and flashy is better than being accurate.

These trends have caught news producers in a culture war between old-school responsible reporting and profitability, as institutions struggle to adapt to the internet. Shams, scams, and spam compete for space with legitimate articles and fakes can look shockingly like the real thing. In the traditional environment the laborious task of fact-checking was done by hand. Few people can spare the time and energy to fact-check every piece of information they come across— not even journalists. Stories that are "too good to check" are rushed off to the presses and the responsibility of verification is left to organizations like Snopes and Politifact. This is how fake news goes viral.

Compounding the problem, studies show that 44 percent of American adults now get at least some of their news from Facebook. But the quality of the news any individual social media user gets often depends not just on the people sharing it, but also the proprietary, black-box algorithms working behind the scenes to determine what ends up in your newsfeed.

Recently, both Google and Facebook have issued assurances that they are working hard to stem the tide and filter fake news now streaming through their respective platforms. Since the presidential election, efforts to combat the spread of misinformation have included publishing a list of fake news sites, while a group of students created a verification browser plug-in at a hackathon. Most of these efforts have concentrated on identifying whether or not an information source is trustworthy, but the adage to "attack the problem at the source" may not prove to be the best strategy for two reasons.

First, websites peddling fake news are created every day; if one gets blacklisted, another will simply take its place. Responding to and maintaining an up-to-date list of websites becomes as onerous as a never-ending game of virtual whack-a-mole. Second, misinformation can spread with alarming speed. News is downloaded, shared and re-shared across many channels. Then, by the time you read it, the fake article has been effectively separated from its originating source, making it almost indistinguishable from actual news. Source verification is just one piece of the fake news puzzle, but content needs to be addressed as well.

Man vs. Machine

In 2015, our team at the University of Western Ontario put out a series of short articles categorizing varieties of fakes and evaluating the role of text analytics. Outright fraudulent news aims to create false conclusions in the reader's mind—often not easy to spot for a human reader. Deceptive writing, it turns out, contains subtle yet detectable language patterns that can be picked up by algorithms. Automated deception detection is an inter-disciplinary field that

Do news stories need to be flashy to get our attention now that we view so much content from our devices?

holds promise in deciphering truthful messages from outright lies based on linguistic patterns and machine learning. Though such methods are rarely applied to news thus far, our 2015 experiments in deception detection in news achieved 63 percent success rates. Human abilities to detect lies are notoriously poorer than that (54 percent on average).

Plus: Machines are tireless and programs are scalable. Humans, on the other hand, are not.

Automated rumor debunking is another field that attempts to identify and prevent the spread of rumors and hoaxes shared over social media, often in real time. Content features are combined with network feature analysis looking, for instance, at users' profiles, locations, and message propagation.

Other varieties of so-called fake news, in the style of comedians like Stephen Colbert or John Oliver, appear harmless. They take on social issues, and aim strictly to entertain—and to the extent that there ever is collateral damage, it is typically a matter of pure misunderstanding: If the joke goes unnoticed, the content is mistaken for real, and then shared ad nauseam. But based on content features like absurdity, humor, and incongruity, we were able to train an algorithm to differentiate this sort of satirical news from legitimate news, achieving 87 percent accuracy in summer 2016.

The satire-detector user interface will be provided shortly for the general public to experiment with. "Every man should have a built-in automatic crap detector operating inside him," Ernest Hemingway was quoted as saying in a 1965 article. "It also should have a manual drill and a crank handle in case the machine breaks down." Fifty years later, the need is greater than ever—and maybe these and similar tools will help.

Of course, all types of text analysis software—from deception-detectors and rumor-debunkers to satire-detectors—are designed to augment our human discernment, rather than replace it, by highlighting which news may warrant more scrutiny. Critical thinking on the part of the readers remains key, and therein lies the real problem. Studies have shown that over 20 percent of adults with university degrees have low literacy proficiency, with the situation much worse in the general population. To exacerbate the issue, many of these adults were educated at a time before the internet had such a strong influence over our lives—some before the World Wide Web was even invented. Information literacy skills are key to navigating the vast, online sea of fake news.

Technologies like our satire detector can help us deal with information overload by automating a certain level of quality control, but ultimately, the most important "crap" detector is the one inside our heads.

EVALUATING THE AUTHORS' ARGUMENTS:

In this viewpoint, Victoria L. Rubin, Yimin Chen, and Niall J. Conroy contend that one of the many problems with the influx of fake news is the information overload we now deal with in the era of the twenty-four-hour news cycle. How can people use both algorithms and critical thinking to determine what are the legitimate news pieces?

We Must Look Beyond the Message We Want to Hear

"The rise of fake news might be one of the lasting legacies of the 2016 election, unless the sites that help it spread take steps to quell its expansion."

Lauren C. Williams

In the following viewpoint, Lauren C. Williams argues that it's not just Facebook, but all digital media that is to blame for the rapid rise of fake news stories being treated as legitimate. The author also examines the more nuanced problem of legitimate sites rushing to publish stories that are only partially true or that have not been properly verified. Because such stories come from legitimate organizations, they are more difficult for consumers to detect and dismiss. Williams is tech reporter at ThinkProgress.

AS YOU READ, CONSIDER THE FOLLOWING QUESTIONS:

1. According to the author, why do readers seek out news sources based on messages they like most, rather than on facts?

2. What happened after Facebook fired its human Trending Topics curators?

3. What happens when Facebook lends legitimacy to fake news social media pages like InfoWars and Politics Insider?

"Fake News Isn't All Facebook's Fault. Sprawling Digital Media Made It Worse," by Lauren C. Williams, ThinkProgress, December 8, 2016. Reprinted by permission.

Fake news got real this weekend after a North Carolina man brandished and fired a rifle in a Washington, D.C. pizza shop. No one was injured or killed, but 28-year-old shooter Edgar Maddison Welch of Salisbury, North Carolina told police he came to "self-investigate" an internet conspiracy theory that suggested Hillary Clinton and her campaign chief John Podesta were involved in a child sex ring run out of the restaurant Comet Ping Pong.

The conspiracy—dubbed #Pizzagate—has been thoroughly debunked, but hasn't stopped high-profile conservatives from promoting the story. Michael G. Flynn Jr., the son and former aide to retired Lt. Gen. Michael Flynn—who was appointed to lead the NSA under the Trump administration—was fired from Trump's transition team after he tweeted that the story hadn't been proven false. That tweet followed one from the elder Flynn containing a link to other dubious claims regarding Clinton.

The rise of fake news might be one of the lasting legacies of the 2016 election, unless the sites that help it spread take steps to quell its expansion. Social media platforms such as Facebook and Twitter share some of the blame, but so do digital journalists and the media at large.

The industry proliferated over the last decade with an infusion of digital-only, niche sites varying in scope and standards as news organizations scrambled to adapt to consumers' increasing desire for online content at the start of President Barack Obama's first term. The shift created congestion, and with so much noise online, it was inevitable for readers to tune out, choosing to trust "news" sources based on the message they liked most, rather than facts.

Facebook has prided itself on letting users drive its content and determine what events or news are most relevant via its infamous algorithm. The site once employed a small editorial staff who helped curate its Trending Topics, the area on the homepage that shows the top news stories being discussed. But the social network fired all of its human curators shortly after a Gizmodo article suggested the site had an anti-conservative news bias when it came to selecting which stories to promote. The allegations galvanized conservative voters and politicians, and Facebook decided to rely solely on its algorithm to feature newsworthy stories. The move has been largely unsuccessful, with false stories frequently featured as Trending Topics based on how many users are interacting with them.

Conveniently, that's also a better way to make money. Facebook—and digital media overall—rely on users' clicks to fuel an ad revenue business that rivals only Google. And until recently, fabricated or unverified stories was a part of that.

After an onslaught of criticism for downplaying the effects of fake news and dismissing his site's culpability, Facebook CEO Mark Zuckerberg said the site would crack down on the spread of fake news with more robust reporting and detection tools, including a third-party verification process.

While Zuckerberg's plan is still in the works, it may not go far enough, since Facebook has already bestowed their blue check mark upon dozens of pages belonging to fake news sites such as InfoWars and Politics Insider, essentially lending legitimacy to their content, boosting their reach by favorably weighting the algorithm, and allowing them to build huge audiences reaching into the millions.

It's unclear if Facebook's new policies would remove the verified badges from online publications which are already verified yet known to promote slanted or unsubstantiated content. (Facebook didn't return requests for comment on its verification process for publications.)

The problem, however, is bigger than Facebook. Yes, nearly half of American adults use social network to get their news, but the ever expanding digital media world is also at fault. Digital-only publications with Congressional press credentials make up 37 percent of the Washington press gallery—a 32 percent jump from 2009 to 2014. That growth led to a 20 percent increase in digital revenue, which in turn motivated traditional and new media organizations to make headlines more punchy. Fold in blogs, native ads, and the proliferation of bogus news sites that host content with false information to chase clicks and ad revenue, and there's a recipe for confusion.

The problem is so bad, one study found, that students were unable to differentiate between story headlines from legitimate news organizations and fake ones. *PC Magazine*'s reporters had a similarly challenging experience parsing facts-only news from misleading takes. On Sunday, what started as a harmless exercise of free speech on

CEO Mark Zuckerberg has been forced to address the problem of fake news on Facebook, which raises the question of whether social media platforms are now in the news business.

social media resulted in ongoing death threats and a criminal shooting at a pizza shop, with passive endorsement of a conspiracy theory from high-ranking officials. It is proof that fabricated, misinformed, or propaganda-laden news has tangible consequences.

The "Different Species" of Fake News

Over three presidential election cycles, social media use among American adults skyrocketed nine times over, from 7 percent in 2005 to 65 percent in 2015. The number of digital news organizations has spiked as well, with many established journalists abandoning long-revered publications such as the *Washington Post* for digital-only shops. That shift has given consumers a plethora of online sources of news—and little guidance on how to tell what's real, slanted, or completely fake.

"Trust in news has been declining for decades," said Deen Freelon, an associate communication studies professor at American

University in Washington, D.C. "Part of this has been an attempt by Republicans and some liberals to blame media for bias. But how do we define fake news? It's important for us to distinguish the different species."

Freelon said some sites publish stories wherein "pieces of it are true, and that can muddy the waters making it difficult to dismiss them offhand. And when stories by reputable news sources are incorrect, or given credence because they are repeated by people in power, they're carrying forth information that is, at best, dubiously sourced because someone in power said it," often without a lot of context judging from a headline.

One example. In late 2012, the *Daily Caller* published the first in a series of articles alleging Sen. Bob Menendez (D-NJ) paid two prostitutes for sex while in the Dominican Republic. The story was a complete fabrication, but the *Daily Caller*'s ceaseless coverage contained enough nuggets of truth to give the rest of the story an air of legitimacy: Menendez did take lavish trips—including to the Dominican Republic—with wealthy donor Salomon Melgen, and failed to declare them as gifts.

FAST FACT

More than a third of US adults polled by YouGov believed the "Pizzagate" story was "probably" or "definitely" true. Even after the story was proven false, doubts lingered.

"The truth is difficult. It's hard to deal with when the truth can go in any direction. It can support what you believe, people you like; it can offend, it can reveal things about people you would rather not know about, or make you uncomfortable," Freelon said. "Sometimes people you don't like have better facts."

"It taxes the average person's ability to tell what's real and what's not. I think it taxes people's critical faculties to the point where they throw their hands up and they fall back on confirmation bias."

That mental exhaustion makes it easier for readers to swallow dubious or misleading headlines in their social media feeds. Then the habit forms: "Consume the information that makes you feel most comfortable, and anytime someone says something you don't like, call them biased," said Freelon.

Comfort in Fake News

The explosion in online content allows consumers to skip the news they don't like and click on the content that makes them feel good.

"At the very basic level, they are making choices in a very different way than they used to when media was limited to a small number of channels," said Pamela Rutledge, a media psychologist and researcher in Newport Beach, California. "When you have those kind of choices, people react in different ways, people choose news that reaffirms their world values."

And consumers don't necessarily consider those stories that confirm their beliefs to be fake. "Those who are against [President Barack] Obama, would find a story questioning his citizenship agreeable because they have negative associations," and are willing to ignore facts or a contradictory story "because it didn't agree with their worldview."

Add that to the fear factor that was present in high doses during the 2016 election, and you have a recipe for consumers to dig into their preconceived notions about the world.

"When you get people scared, people retreat from opposing views," Rutledge said. "The more you fire people up with fear—we saw that on both sides in this election—the more likely people are going to look for information that reaffirms their world views. You need to be right because you're scared. You want to be able to control that uncertainty."

Fear and rationality utilize two different parts of the brain, Rutledge said. "That drives how people seek out news and why they're willing to believe things that if you look at the logic of it don't make any sense at all."

Making News Human Again

Fake news isn't a new problem and it likely won't go away on its own, but solving it won't be simple.

"Part of the issue we have to deal with does involve Facebook, because their algorithm decides what people consume, and people aren't consuming news on their own terms. Facebook is privileging news from sources with tenuous relationships with the truth," Freelon said.

"Facebook has tried to have it both ways by making the editorial decision that [the company's employees] aren't responsible for what people consume but depend on that consumption" for ad revenue, he continued.

In a perfect world, Freelon said, Facebook would "commit to publishing content seeking the truth, correcting stories when they are incorrect, and downplaying those that don't." But that counters Facebook's current business model, and would likely require the company to take an active role in what links and stories are pushed up by its algorithm.

The answer to fake news' persistence will likely be a crowdsourced effort with consumers, fact-checking organizations, and journalists vetting news through its source—checking to see if a domain is new, or a site is underdeveloped, Freelon said.

Developers have already launched a browser extension in the wake of Facebook's fake news scandal. The Chrome plugin "Fake News Alert" flags sites that could be hoaxes, satire, or questionably sourced, based on a now-viral list of sites Merrimack College communications professor Melissa Zimdars compiled for her students.

"Removing the burden from the individual to crowdsourcing the veracity of sites would be incredibly helpful," said Freelon. "You can't prevent people from consuming fake news, but you can make it so that when they do it, it's willingly and with fair warning."

And while the sheer volume of media wears on consumers' ability to decipher fact from fiction, from analysis, or from opinion, Rutledge believes traditional news organizations can help.

"Humanize people on all sides of these stories," she said. "It's really easy to make an 'other' class of people—immigrants or bankers, people see them as the same things."

"What this election has done is raise the issue everywhere. That works in favor of the traditional news sites because they have legitimacy," she said. Referring to her students, "I have kids who cite Wikipedia as an official source because they've never been taught to think about how these things are created."

Viewpoint

4

Forget Click-Bait and Support Real Journalism

"Increasingly, content isn't created by journalists once employed by legacy media. It comes from freelancers, citizen journalists, bloggers and vloggers."

Jeffrey Dvorkin

In the following viewpoint, Jeffrey Dvorkin argues that digital technology is responsible for the current crisis and inevitable downfall of traditional journalism. The author believes that journalism is becoming "Uber-ized," a part of the gig economy where content is being created by cheaper freelancers, citizen journalists, bloggers, and vloggers, who are not as trained or as experienced as the older, traditional journalists. Dvorkin was vice president of news and information at NPR and is director of the journalism program at the University of Toronto.

AS YOU READ, CONSIDER THE FOLLOWING QUESTIONS:

1. Per the viewpoint, why doesn't journalism pay anymore?

2. Why do digital media companies try to entice their audiences through "click-bait"?

3. According to the author, what does journalism have to do to survive in digital culture?

"Column: Why Click-Bait Will Be the Death of Journalism," by Jeffrey Dvorkin, NewsHour Productions LLC, April 27, 2016. Reprinted by permission.

J ournalism is (once again) in crisis. This time, the sky really does seem to be falling.

Newspapers are losing readers and revenue. Some are shutting down all over North America. In Canada, it has been particularly acute, with the largest chain consolidating newsrooms in two-newspaper markets in January. Long-established small town newspapers in Ontario and British Columbia have simply vanished overnight after more than a century of service. Broadcasters continue to shrink, even as local U.S. TV stations in caucus and primary states make their usual profits in an ad-rich election year. Canadian TV stations are threatening to shut their local news operations unless a better model is found.

When the Solution Is Actually the Problem

Media managers are wondering what went wrong. Reporters and editors are asking why journalism doesn't pay any more. However, if simple solutions are hard to discern, the media have only to look at the technology they once so eagerly embraced.

It's the digital technology. It emerged in the late 1990s and early 2000s and swept through every aspect of modern life, including journalism. As ratings and circulation declined, media organizations, pressured by shareholders and desperate to find a way to return to the great profit margins of the 1980s, seized on digital as the silver bullet of transformations.

But if ever there was a double-edged sword, it is the digital culture. It has enlarged our informational possibilities while at the same time offering up trivia like cat videos, celebrity sightings and "listicles." It is, in effect, driving journalistic deviance downward, to paraphrase Daniel Patrick Moynihan.

Yet media organizations stubbornly insist that digital is the solution. They cling to digital like a torpedoed sailor clings to a raft, hoping that the submarine won't hit them again.

In February in Toronto, at a gathering sponsored by the Canadian Journalism Foundation, three prominent newspaper publishers (Montreal's La Presse, the Toronto Globe and Mail and the Toronto Star) discussed the future of the business. To a person, they were all

Several grassroots news organizations, such as the Conversation, have emerged to return focus to solid journalism with integrity.

bullish. And that future for newspapers, they said, is digital, digital and more digital.

We live in strange times.

- We have a lodging system called Airbnb. It doesn't own any actual hotels.
- There's a food delivery service called Foodora. It doesn't own any restaurants.
- There's a video service called YouTube. It doesn't produce movies.
- There's a taxi company called Uber. It doesn't own any cars.

Journalism is also being Uber-ized. Increasingly, content isn't created by journalists once employed by legacy media. It comes from freelancers, citizen journalists, bloggers and vloggers. Freelancers are being hired while experienced, older journalists are laid off. In the rush to return to the once-rich profit margins of the early 2000s, media organizations are being urged by their shareholders to dispense with expensive ventures like international reporting. Newspapers have closed or been downsized, broadcasters have cut their more expensive (and more labor-intensive) content. News consultants like Frank N. Magid Associates are hired to tell their news clients that weather, traffic and crime, or WTC, are what most audiences prefer.

Not coincidentally, WTC also happens to be the cheapest and most readily available content. And all three bits of low-hanging journalistic fruit originate from government sources: weather from the National Weather Service (Environment Canada based in Ottawa), traffic reports from various Department of Transportations at the state and provincial levels and, of course, crime from local police forces. (The last of these may have a financial incentive to make sure that the media reports as much criminal activity as possible, even when crime rates are declining.)

So much for independent journalistic inquiry. And studies are showing that all three of the WTCs evoke strong feelings of anxiety in audiences. The news seems to be in the business of producing "moral panic."

It's not all bad. Many businesses have been properly transformed and modernized by digital. While customers have benefited from the ease, cost-effectiveness and simplicity of digital, there is also a powerful downside: Wages for workers in those industries have plummeted (journalism included), working conditions are often worse, and company morale, in many instances, is still dropping and has not yet hit rock bottom. Journalists' unions seem particularly ineffective under these circumstances, accepting downsizing and reduced salaries, because they understand their choices and influence are limited to say the least.

The Quest for Clicks

At the same time, profit margins in many industries have never been greater. Media organizations with smaller labor-intensive operations are doing well, and startups are being courted by Wall Street IPOs. (Buzzfeed raised $850 million last year in order to get into the news and film business and away from cat videos and listicles.)

This increased competition from media organizations like Buzzfeed, Vice Media and Vox have put renewed pressure on legacy media. Broadcasters especially try to entice their audiences through click-bait. This is defined as "an [eye-catching] link on a website which encourages people to read on. It is often paid for by the advertiser ('Paid' click-bait) or generates income based on the number of clicks."

It's rarely newsworthy, but it does attract eyeballs. The assumption seems to be that audiences might stay for the "serious" content after gorging on the fluff. The public broadcaster in Canada, the CBC, seems to be particularly smitten with click-bait, even though its own journalists complain, and the public resents this waste of the public broadcaster's journalistic efforts and reputation.

No technological change can ever be reversed. Occasionally, it can be slowed, even questioned. Can the effects of the digital culture be made to work on behalf of the culture rather than against it? If journalism is to survive, it has to resist digital's worst qualities in order to let it offer what's best on behalf of the public.

Digital is merely a technology, like the telephone. It's a technology that will only thrive if it has something of value to transmit. But anxious media managers seem to have become believers in a technology possessed with apparent magical properties.

One of the best qualities in the journalistic culture is skepticism. But when it comes to digital, skepticism has been replaced with unquestioning enthusiasm. And the information-starved public is being left behind.

EVALUATING THE AUTHOR'S ARGUMENTS:

In this viewpoint, Jeffrey Dvorkin argues that traditional news is simply not as exciting as the topics covered in "click-bait" stories, and that factors into the downfall of "serious" content. With the continuing expansion of digital media, how can journalists who write "serious" content make their stories more appealing to today's reader?

Facts About Internet Journalism and Fake News

Editor's note: These facts can be used in reports to add credibility when making important points or claims.

Per Merriam-Webster, "fake news" is frequently used to describe a political story that is seen as damaging to an agency, entity, or person.

According to Google Trends, the term "fake news" reached its peak interest during the week of January 8–14, 2017. Prior to the first major spike in popularity, November 13–19, 2016, the last popularity spike happened during the week of July 14–20, 2013.

Major newspapers began creating online websites in the early 1990s.

In 2015, 55 percent of people reported that print was their preferred method for reading a newspaper, down 4 percent from 2014.

The first type of digital journalism, called teletext, was invented in the UK in 1970.

In the late 1980s and early 1990s, smaller newspaper entities started online news services using Bulletin Board Systems software. The first was the *Albuquerque Tribune* in 1989.

In September 1992, *Computer Gaming World* broke the news of Electronic Arts' acquisition of Origin Systems on the site Prodigy, prior to the hard copy issue going to press.

In 1980, approximately 20,000 people around the world had access to the internet by way of 200 university, military, and government host computers.

In 1980, the *New York Times* Infobank database system began offering its stories in full-text form.

Per Statista, in 2015, the number of full-time newspaper journalists in the United States was 32,900, down from 41,600 in 2011.

Early internet forums were described as a web version of an electronic mailing list or newsgroup, such as Usenet. One of the first forum sites that is still active today is Delphi Forums, which dates to 1983.

According to a study from Carnegie Mellon University, 57 percent of respondents preferred to remain anonymous when participating in special interest groups, while 55 percent of respondents preferred to remain anonymous while social networking.

Fifty-five percent of Americans have posted an online comment and 78 percent have read comments, according to a report released in 2016 at SXSW by the Engaging News Project.

In the three months before the 2016 US presidential election, pro-Trump fabricated stories tracked by the researchers were shared a total of 30 million times. This is nearly quadruple the number of pro-Clinton shares.

According to NPR Ethics, transparency is used to inspire confidence in journalism: "We reveal as much as we practically can about how we discover and verify the facts we present. We strive to make our decision-making process clear to the public, especially when we find ourselves wrestling with tough choices. We disclose any relationships, whether with partners or funders, that might appear to influence our coverage."

Organizations to Contact

The editors have compiled the following list of organizations concerned with the issues debated in this book. The descriptions are derived from materials provided by the organizations. All have publications or information available for interested readers. The list was compiled on the date of publication of the present volume; the information provided here may change. Be aware that many organizations take several weeks or longer to respond to inquiries, so allow as much time as possible for the receipt of requested materials.

AlterNet
77 Federal Street, Second Floor
San Francisco, CA 94107
(415) 284-1420
website: www.alternet.org
AlterNet is an award-winning news magazine and online community that creates original journalism and amplifies the best of hundreds of other independent media sources. AlterNet's aim is to inspire action and advocacy on the environment, human rights and civil liberties, social justice, media, health care issues, and more.

Cato Institute
1000 Massachusetts Avenue NW
Washington, DC 20001-5403
(202) 842-0200
email: cato@cato.org
website: www.cato.org
The Cato Institute is a public policy research organization—a think tank—dedicated to the principles of individual liberty, limited government, free markets, and peace. Its scholars and analysts conduct independent, nonpartisan research on a wide range of policy issues.

Center for American Progress
1333 H Street NW, 10th Floor
Washington, DC 20005
(202) 682-1611
website: www.americanprogress.org
The Center for American Progress is an independent nonpartisan policy institute that is dedicated to improving the lives of all Americans through bold, progressive ideas, as well as strong leadership and concerted action.

The International Consortium of Investigative Journalists
910 17th Street NW, Suite 410
Washington, DC 20006
website: www.icij.org
The International Consortium of Investigative Journalists is a global network of more than 190 investigative journalists in more than 65 countries who collaborate on in-depth investigative stories. Founded in 1997 by the respected American journalist Chuck Lewis, ICIJ was launched as a project of the Center for Public Integrity to extend the center's style of watchdog journalism, focusing on issues that do not stop at national frontiers: cross-border crime, corruption, and the accountability of power.

The Nieman Foundation for Journalism at Harvard University
One Francis Avenue
Cambridge, MA 02138
(617) 495-2237
email: staff@nicmanlab.org
website: www.niemanlab.org
The Nieman Journalism Lab is an attempt to help journalism figure out its future in an internet age. It wants to help reporters and editors adjust to their online labors, it wants to help traditional news organizations find a way to survive, and it wants to help the new crop of startups that will complement—or supplant—them.

Online News Association

1111 North Capitol Street NE, Sixth Floor
Washington, DC 20002
(202) 503-9222
email: irving@journalists.org
website: www.journalists.org
The Online News Association is the world's largest association of digital journalists. ONA's mission is to inspire innovation and excellence among journalists to better serve the public.

Pew Research Center

1615 L Street NW, Suite 800
Washington, DC 20036
(202) 419-4300
email: info@pewresearch.org
website: www.pewresearch.org
Pew Research Center is a nonpartisan fact tank that informs the public about the issues, attitudes, and trends shaping America and the world. It conducts public opinion polling, demographic research, content analysis, and other data-driven social science research.

Society of Professional Journalists

3909 N. Meridian Street
Indianapolis, IN 46208
(317) 927-8000
email: agutierrez@spj.org
website: www.spj.org
The Society of Professional Journalists is the nation's most broad-based journalism organization, dedicated to encouraging the free practice of journalism and stimulating high standards of ethical behavior. Founded in 1909 as Sigma Delta Chi, SPJ promotes the free flow of information vital to a well-informed citizenry through the daily work of its nearly 7,500 members, works to inspire and educate current and future journalists through professional development, and protects First Amendment guarantees of freedom of speech and press through its advocacy efforts.

For Further Reading

Books

Atton, Chris, and James F. Hamilton. *Alternative Journalism*. Los Angeles, CA: SAGE, 2008. Investigates and analyzes the diverse forms and genres of journalism that have arisen as challenges to mainstream news coverage. This exploration goes to the heart of journalism itself, prompting a critical inquiry into the epistemology of news, the professional norms of objectivity, the elite basis of journalism, and the hierarchical commerce of news production.

Garrison, Bruce. *Computer-Assisted Reporting*. Mahwah, NJ: Lawrence Earlbaum Associates, Publishers, 1998. Focuses on the computerization of newsgathering. It highlights how computers assists journalists by making writing easier, simplifies gathering and organization, and proposes five stages for the development of computer literacy in the newsroom.

Gillmor, Dan. *We the Media: Grassroots Journalism By the People, For the People*. Sebastopol, CA: O'Reilly Media, 2004. Discusses how grassroots internet journalists have changed the way news is handled. A major point is how big media corporations can no longer control the news now that it is being published in real-time and widely available via the internet.

King, Elliot. *Free for All: The Internet's Transformation of Journalism*. Evanston, IL: Northwestern University Press, 2010. Scholar Elliot King covers a brief history of journalism and the development of new media, beginning with the appearance of newspapers in the sixteenth century. *Free for All* provides anyone with an interest in the future of journalism the grounding necessary for an informed discussion.

Lindner, Ken. *The New Broadcasting Realities*. Cleveland, OH: Live Oak Book Company, 2011. An insider's look at the world of broadcasting. Lindner offers solutions to the complex issues and problems broadcasting professionals face in today's media landscape.

Mott, Frank Luther. *American Journalism: A History of Newspapers in the United States Through 250 Years, 1690-1940*. London, UK:

Routledge/Thoemmes. A history of the newspapers in the United States through 250 Years: 1690 to 1940.

Stephens, Mitchell. *Beyond News: The Future of Journalism*. New York, NY: Columbia University Press, 2014. Proposes a new standard for journalism, "wisdom journalism," an amalgam of the more rarified forms of reporting—exclusive, enterprising, investigative—and informed, insightful, interpretive, explanatory, even opinionated takes on current events. It emphasizes how mindsets need to change to focus on what journalism can become in a digital world.

Vaughn, Stephen L. *Encyclopedia of American Journalism*. London, UK: Routledge, 2008. Explores the history of journalism in the United States in print media, radio, television, and the internet. Documents the integral part that journalism has played in the formation of American culture, covering key figures and moments in the history of American Journalism.

Periodicals and Internet Sources

Allcott, Hunt, and Matthew Gentzkow. "Social Media and Fake News in the 2016 Election," *Journal of Economic Perspectives*, January 2017.

Barthel, Michael, and Amy Mitchell. "Americans' Attitudes About the News Media Deeply Divided Along Partisan Lines," Pew Research Center, May 10, 2017. http://www.journalism.org/2017/05/10/americans-attitudes-about-the-news-media-deeply-divided-along-partisan-lines/.

Barthel, Michael, Amy Mitchell, and Jess Holcomb. "Many Americans Believe Fake News Is Sowing Confusion," *Pew Research Center*, December 15, 2016. http://www.journalism.org/2016/12/15/many-americans-believe-fake-news-is-sowing-confusion/.

Brown, Ian, and Douwe Korff. "Digital Freedoms in International Law," *Global Network Initiative*, June 14, 2012. https://globalnetworkinitiative.org/sites/default/files/Digital%20Freedoms%20in%20International%20Law.pdf.

Elizabeth, Jane. "When Facts Don't Make a Difference: 4 Good Questions with Brendan Nyhan," *American Press Institute*, May 29, 2014. https://www.americanpressinstitute.org/fact-checking-project/facts-dont-make-difference-4-good-questions-brendan-nyhan/.

Gottfried, Jeffrey, Michael Barthel, and Amy Mitchell. "Trump, Clinton Voters Divided in Their Main Source for Election News," *Pew Research Center*, January 18, 2017. http://www.journalism .org/2017/01/18/trump-clinton-voters-divided-in-their-main -source-for-election-news/.

Greenwald, Glenn. "NSA Collecting Phone Records of Millions of Verizon Customers Daily," *Guardian*, June 6, 2013. https://www .theguardian.com/world/2013/jun/06/nsa-phone-records-verizon -court-order.

Holan, Angie Drobnic. "2016 Lie of the Year: Fake News," *PolitiFact*, December 13, 2016. http://www.politifact.com/truth-o-meter /article/2016/dec/13/2016-lie-year-fake-news/.

Kovach, Bill, and Tom Rosenstiel. "Blur: How to Know What's True in the Age of Information Overload," *Bloomsbury*, 2011.

Marx, Gary T. "What's in a Name? Some Reflections on the Sociology of Anonymity," *The Information Society*, 1999.

Nyhan, Brendan. "Fact-Checking Can Change Views? We Rate That as Mostly True," *TheUpshot*, November 5, 2016. https://www.nytimes .com/2016/11/06/upshot/fact-checking-can-change-views-we-rate -that-as-mostly-true.html?rref=collection%2Fsectioncollection %2Fupshot&action=click&contentCollection=upshot&region= stream&module=stream_unit&version=search&content Placement=1&pgtype=sectionfront.

Owen, Bruce. "Old Media Policy Failures, New Media Policy Challenges," *Stanford Institute for Economic Policy Research*, June 2009.

Pew. "State of the News Media," *Pew Research Institute*, 2017. http:// www.pewresearch.org/topics/state-of-the-news-media/.

Rosen, Jay. "Bloggers vs. Journalists Is Over," *PressThink*, January 21, 2005. http://archive.pressthink.org/2005/01/21/berk_essy.html.

Scacco, Joshua. "General Election News Coverage: What Engages Audiences Down the Ballot," *Engaging News Project,* April 2017.

Schneier, Bruce. "NSA Surveillance: A Guide to Staying Secure," *Guardian*, September 6, 2013. https://www.theguardian.com/world/2013/ sep/05/nsa-how-to-remain-secure-surveillance.

Stroud, Natalie Jomini, et al. "Journalist Involvement in Comment Sections," *Engaging News Project*, April 2014.

Websites

NPR (www.npr.org)
The mission of NPR is to work in partnership with member stations to create a more informed public—one challenged and invigorated by a deeper understanding and appreciation of events, ideas, and cultures. To accomplish its mission, NPR produces, acquires, and distributes programming that meets the highest standards of public service in journalism and cultural expression.

PolitiFact (www.politifact.com)
PolitiFact is a fact-checking website that rates the accuracy of claims by elected officials and others who speak up in American politics. PolitiFact is run by editors and reporters from the *Tampa Bay Times*, an independent newspaper in Florida, as is PunditFact, a site devoted to fact-checking pundits.

Poynter (www.poynter.org)
The Poynter Institute is the world's leading instructor, innovator, convener, and resource for journalists and citizens in twenty-first century democracies. Poynter teaches management, ethical decision-making, editing, writing, reporting, and new media skills.

Snopes (www.snopes.com)
Snopes was founded in 1994 by David Mikkelson and is the largest fact-checking site on the internet. The Snopes.com website is (and always has been) a completely independent, self-sufficient entity wholly owned by its operators and funded through advertising revenues.

Society of Professional Journalists (www.spj.org)
The Society of Professional Journalists is dedicated to the perpetuation of a free press as the cornerstone of our nation and our liberty. It provides a definition for the role of journalists, that they provide information in an accurate, comprehensive, timely, and understandable manner.

Index

A

advertising, 8, 18, 83, 105

Allcott, Hunt, 74–75

American Press Institute, 81

America Online, 11, 14

anonymity, 10–16, 27, 31, 32, 35–39, 58

anonymous sources, 31–33, 35–39

API's Fact-Checking Project, 81, 82, 83, 84

Appelbaum, Jacob, 25

Associated Press, 7, 37, 84

automated rumor debunking, 91

B

bin Laden, Osama, 43

blogs/bloggers, 15, 19, 20, 26, 29, 35, 69, 95, 103

breaking news, 36, 49, 51

British Airways flight 77, 43

British Anti-Terror Law, 25

Buzzfeed, 8, 54, 55, 74, 104, 105

C

Canadian news, 102–103

Center for News Literacy, 86

Christie, Chris, 38

Christopherson, Elizabeth Good, 84

CIA, 41–43, 45

citizen journalism, 17–21, 23, 101, 103

Clark, Jessica, 87

click-bait, 8, 101, 105

Clinton, Hillary, 55, 57, 74, 75, 94

CNN, 55, 69

Colbert, Stephen, 91

Comet Ping Pong, 93

comment posting, 59–61, 63

Communications Decency Act, 14

Conway, Kellyanne, 57

Corbett, Phil, 37

D

Daily Caller, 97

Democrats, 57

digital-only publications, 95, 96

E

Engaging News Project, 60

ethics, 7, 12, 48, 49

F

Facebook, 45, 70
  ad revenue, 95
  algorithm, 8
  and fake news sites, 65, 71, 72, 74, 89, 93, 94, 95, 99
  as news source, 8, 41, 42–43, 44, 46, 75, 89
  Trending Topics, 8, 93, 94–95

fact-checking, 47, 66–70, 71, 74, 79, 81–84, 87, 89, 99

FactCheck.org, 65, 71
fake news
  cause of, 93–100
  comfort in, 98
  compared to unverified
    news, 54–58
  fight against, 79–81, 83–87,
    88–92
  how to spot, 64–71
Fake News Alert plugin, 99
"false balance," 51
financial crisis of 2008, 23–24
Flynn, Michael, 93
Flynn, Michael G., Jr., 94
Foster, Vince, 55
Founding Fathers, 10, 13, 14
freedom of speech, 14, 28
Freelon, Deen, 97–98, 99
FSB, 57

G
Gentzkow, Matthew, 74–76
Gillmor, Dan, 23, 27
Glaisyer, Tom, 85–86
global warming, 51
Google, 29, 65, 72, 90, 95
Greenwald, Glenn, 23–27
Grenier, Robert, 42
Guardian, 20, 21, 23, 26, 27, 43

H
Hemingway, Ernest, 92

I
InfoWars, 95
internet
  and anonymity, 10–16

and citizen journalism, 18–21
culture, 11
effect on news reporting and
    consumption, 41–47, 89
false information on, 81, 86
forums, 11, 14, 15
and media change, 18–19,
    22–30
and online news, 11
investigative reporters, 40–47
ISIS, 38, 74

J
Jarvis, Jeff, 15
journalism
  and activism, 23–26
  and anonymous sources,
    31–33, 35–39
  balance and fairness in,
    48–49, 51–52
  citizen, 17–21, 23, 101, 103
  crisis and downfall
    of, 101–105
  ethics, 32–33, 35–39, 49
  role in the media, 23–28
  and social media, 27
  surveillance, 28, 29
  and technology, 27–29
  transparency and account-
    ability, 35–37

K
Kaplan, David E., 44
Keller, Bill, 26
Khashoggi, Jamal, 43
Kiesa, Abby, 86–87
Kovach, Bill, 80

Kramer, Larry, 87
Kremlin, 56–57

L
Lehman Brothers, 23
Lewis, Paul, 43–44
listicles, 8, 102, 104

M
Macedonia, 80
Marx, Gary, 12, 15
mass media
  and click-bait, 95, 101–105
  companies, 18–19, 21, 31
  and fake news, 79, 94, 99
  and the internet, 18–19, 22–30
  recommended best prac-
    tices for, 32
  trust in, 84
McLuhan, Marshall, 12
media criticism, 26
Media Insight Project, 84
Melgen, Salomon, 97
Menendez, Bob, 97
Miranda, David, 25
Mubenga, Jimmy, 43

N
national crime rate, 83–84
news commenter demograph-
  ics, 60–61, 63
news literacy education, 86–87
newspapers
  best practices, 32
  fall in popularity, 102, 103
  online presence, 10, 11,
    14–15, 19, 23, 103

news websites and ano-
  nymity, 10–16
New Voices: New Jersey, 85
New York Times, 7, 26, 31–39, 83
NPR, 20
NSA, 23, 24, 27, 94
Nyhan, Brendan, 83, 84

O
Obama, Barack, 37, 55, 66, 67,
  68, 70, 94, 98
Oliver, John, 91
Omidyar, Pierre, 27
Onion, 7, 54, 55
online forum identity
  models, 15–16
Organized Crime and
  Corruption Reporting Project
  (OCCRP), 44, 45–46

P
PC Magazine, 95–96
People, 71
Pew Research Center's
  Project for Excellence in
  Journalism, 81
Pizzagate, 55, 93, 96, 97
Podesta, John, 93
Poitras, Laura, 24–25
Politics Insider, 95
Politifact, 71, 74, 89
post-truth, 84, 89
Poynter Institute, 12
presidential race of 2012, 83
presidential race of 2016, 73,
  74–75, 80, 81, 82, 83, 84,
  88, 89, 94, 98

ProPublica, 46, 84
pseudonyms, 10, 11, 12, 13,
    14, 15, 54
Putin, Vladimir, 56, 57, 58, 69

Q
Qaeda, al-, 43

R
Radu, Paul Cristian, 45–46
Republicans, 38, 71, 83, 97
Reuters, 7, 37
Rita Allen Foundation, 81, 84
Rosen, Jay, 18
Rosenstiel, Tom, 80–81,
    84, 85, 87
Russia, 55, 56, 57, 80
Rutledge, Pamela, 98, 99

S
satire detector, 92
Schmitt, Eric, 38
Schneier, Bruce, 29
Schumer, Amy, 71
Silver, Sheldon, 38
Snopes.com, 65, 67, 68,
    71, 74, 89
Snowden, Edward, 23–26
social media
    commenting on news stories
        via, 52, 60–61, 63
    and fake news, 65, 74,
        91, 94, 96–98
    and free speech, 96
    and journalists, 41–47
    as news platforms, 41, 45–46,
        75, 89–90, 95, 96–97

role in elections, 74,
    75, 80, 94
Society of Professional
    Journalists, 7, 32
Supreme Court, 8, 10, 14

T
television news, 73–75, 77
three Cs of journalism, 47
Tomlinson, Ian, 43–44
Trad, Faisal al-, 43
Trump, Donald, 55–58, 67,
    68–71, 74–75, 83–84
Trump dossier, 8, 55, 57
truth scale, 83
Twitter, 20, 41, 43–46, 49,
    60, 83, 94

U
unverified news, 54–58, 88, 95
US Border Patrol, 25
US drone program, 38
Usenet, 11
US Strategy for Pakistan and
    Afghanistan conference, 42

V
Verizon, 23
Vice Media, 105
Vox, 105

W
Wall Street Journal, 46
Washington Post Fact
    Checker, 71
Watergate, 26
Welch, Edgar Maddison, 94

whistleblowers, 22, 23,
   36, 39, 44
Woodward, Bob, 26
World Blog Expo, 20
WTC (weather, traffic,
   crime), 104

Y
Yale University, 51
YouTube, 20, 103

Z
Zuckerberg, Mark, 71, 95

Picture Credits